Living in Japan made easy

日本語を学ぶ

日常生活の
会話＆情報

英語を学ぶ

CD付

角田實 著

SANSHUSHA

はじめに

外国人のみなさん，ようこそ日本へ。今あなたは日本の生活を楽しんでいらっしゃいますか？　もし楽しくなかったら，それはたいへんです。

せっかく日本にきたのですから，ぜひ日本に溶け込んでください。それにはまず，やさしい日本語を覚え，積極的に日本人と親しくなりましょう。世界中で日本語はとてもむずかしい言語といわれていますが，それは違います。日本語ではなく，いままでの日本語の教科書がむずかしいのです。

言葉は人間が生きていくための必要最小限の表現を覚えれば，あとは自然に上達します。はじめから学問的に勉強する必要はないのです。とにかく，日本語はやさしくて，面白くなければいけません。

この本は，日本人がよく使う言い回しを集め，外国人にすぐ役立つように工夫されています。さらに日本で生活するために必要な情報をたくさん盛り込みました。これは逆に，いつも外国人に接している日本人にもきっと役に立ちます。

本書の使い方

本書は，日本にきて間もない外国人が必要とする，日本語会話と日本で生活するために必要な情報を，10章構成で74の場面に分けて説明してあります。

各場面は，次の3項目で構成されています。

1.キーセンテンス

各場面でポイントとなる文と，その文が使われる状況を説明しました。

2.ダイアローグ

会話の中にはキーセンテンスが必ず使われています。Jは日本人，Fは外国人の設定になっています。全ての文例にはローマ字をつけてあります。ローマ字は16ページのローマ字表を参考にしてください。

3.コラム

形式にこだわりがちな日本人の生活にとけ込むのに必要と思われる情報を載せました。

また，各章末および巻末には，本文で十分に触れることができなかった情報を掲載しました。こちらも活用してください。

すべての日本語に，英語訳をつけました。日本語を覚ようとする外国人だけでなく，いつも外国人に接している日本人，これから外国人を迎えようとしている方にも役立てていただけると思います。

How to use this book

The 10 chapters of this book are designed to explain necessary (important) information about daily Japanese conversation for foreigners who have just assumed residence in Japan. Altogether, the 10 chapters are divided into 74 skits to exemplify the main points. Each skit has been divided into three sections.

1. Key Sentence

In each skit a key sentence is provided along with an explanation in which the key sentence can be used.

2. Dialog

A dialog that can be used in daily situations is provided in each lesson. The key sentence is used in each dialog.

'J' represents the Japanese and 'F' represents foreigners. The dialog is written in both Japanese script and Roman letters. The Roman letters are provided directly below the Japanese script to indicate the way in which the Japanese script is read. Please turn to page 16 and have a look at an orthography list when you want to read.

3. Column

Important information for living a successful life in Japan is provided. Various subjects have been selected to help make your life in Japan easier and help you get along with Japanese people who are apt to stick to formalities.

In addition, those points that were not fully explained in each column are given further attention at the end of each chapter as well as at the end of the book. So please make use of it.

Each sentence written in Japanese has been translated into English. It is my hope that this book can be of use to not only those foreigners trying to learn the Japanese language but also to those Japanese who are in constant communication with foreigners as well as people who entertain guests from other countries.

目　次

本書の使い方……………………………………………2

第1章　あいさつ

（1）はじめまして。……………………………………18
（2）こんにちは。………………………………………20
（3）はい[ええ]。いいえ。……………………………22
（4）もういちど。すみません。………………………24
（5）しつれいします。…………………………………26
（6）ありがとうございます。…………………………28
（7）さようなら。………………………………………30
あなたの「干支」はなんですか。………………………32

第2章　住まいを定める

（8）駅はどこですか。…………………………………34
（9）アパートを探しています。………………………36
（10）ここを貸してください。…………………………38
（11）外国人登録に来ました。…………………………40
（12）初めて来ました。…………………………………42
（13）こどもの学校のことで来ました。………………44
（14）ゴミの日はいつですか。…………………………46
（15）こんど越してきました。…………………………48
数え方……………………………………………………50

第3章　仕事を探す

（16）広告を見ました。…………………………………52
（17）よろしくお願いします。…………………………54
（18）いまの日本語わかりません。……………………56

CONTENTS

How to use this book ······ 3

I Greeting

(1) How do you do? ······ 19
(2) *Konnichiwa*. (Hello.) ······ 21
(3) *Hai*. (Yes). *Iie*. (No). ······ 23
(4) Could you say that again? ······ 25
(5) Excuse me. (Thank you.) ······ 27
(6) Thank you very much. ······ 29
(7) Good-bye. ······ 31
What is your Chinese birth sign? ······ 32

II Settling down

(8) Where is the station? ······ 35
(9) I'm looking for an apartment house. ······ 37
(10) I'd like to rent this room. ······ 39
(11) I've come to register as a foreign resident. ······ 41
(12) This is my first time to come here. ······ 43
(13) I've come to inquire about a school for my child. ······ 45
(14) Which day should I put out the garbage/trash? ······ 47
(15) I've moved in recently. ······ 49
Counting ······ 50

III Job hunting

(16) I saw your advertisement. ······ 53
(17) *Yoroshiku onegai shimasu*. ······ 55
(18) I don't understand that Japanese phrase very well. ······ 57

（19） 日本語学校に行ってます。……………………………………58
（20） 2年は，いるつもりです。……………………………………60
（21） どんな仕事ですか。……………………………………………62
（22） 明日からでもいいです。………………………………………64
（23） 車の修理をしていました。……………………………………66
（24） あのー，給料日はいつですか。………………………………68
職業の種類……………………………………………………………70

第4章　毎日の生活

（25） おはようございます。…………………………………………72
（26） ただいま。………………………………………………………74
（27） こんばんは。……………………………………………………76
（28） これでいいですか。……………………………………………78
（29） いま，何時ですか。……………………………………………80
（30） これはなんですか。……………………………………………82
（31） おいそがしいですか。…………………………………………84
（32） どういたしまして。……………………………………………86
銀行自動入出金機……………………………………………………88

第5章　交通機関の利用

（33） JRの地図はありますか。……………………………………90
（34） 渋谷までいくらですか。………………………………………92
（35） 池袋に行きますか。……………………………………………94
（36） どうしたらいいですか。………………………………………96
日本の地図……………………………………………………………98

第6章　買い物・外食

（37） ツナの缶詰はありますか。……………………………………100

(19) I go to a Japanese language school. ······ 59
(20) I'm going to stay here for 2 years. ······ 61
(21) What exactly does the job entail? ······ 63
(22) I can start from tomorrow. ······ 65
(23) I was a car repairman. ······ 67
(24) Well, which day is payday? ······ 69
Occupations ······ 70

IV Everyday life

(25) Good morning. ······ 73
(26) I'm back. ······ 75
(27) Good evening. ······ 77
(28) Is this alright? ······ 79
(29) What time is it now? ······ 81
(30) What is this? ······ 83
(31) Are you busy? ······ 85
(32) You're welcome. (Not at all.) ······ 87
Automatic Teller Machine ······ 88

V Using public transport

(33) Could I have a JR map? ······ 91
(34) How much is it to Shibuya? ······ 93
(35) Do you go to Ikebukuro? (Does this bus go to Ikebukuro?) 95
(36) How should I go about it? ······ 97
Map of Japan ······ 98

VI Shopping and eating out

(37) Do you have any canned tuna? ······ 101

(38) やっぱり，これにします。……102
(39) カメラを買(か)いたいのですが。……104
(40) メニューありますか。……106
(41) これはとてもおいしいですね。……108
(42) もっとください。……110
(43) もうおなかいっぱいです。……112
料理(りょうり)の用語(ようご)……114

第7章　つきあい

(44) ごめんください。……116
(45) どうぞ。どうも。……118
(46) いただきます。……120
(47) もう，けっこうです。……122
(48) わー，うれしい。……124
(49) おじゃましました。……126
(50) では，お元気(げんき)で。……128
日本人(にほんじん)の名字(みょうじ)と名前(なまえ)……130

第8章　日本(にほん)を知(し)る

(51) 歌舞伎(かぶき)を見(み)にいきました。……132
(52) 日本(にほん)は美(うつく)しい国(くに)ですね。……134
(53) おめでとうございます。……136
(54) ううん，あんまり。……138
(55) あー，びっくりした。……140
(56) とってもかわいい。……142
(57) なぜ。……144
(58) それで，どうしたの。……146
日本(にほん)の祝祭日(しゅくさいじつ)……148

(38) I'll take this. ············ 103

(39) I'd like to buy a camera. ············ 105

(40) Could I see the menu, please? ············ 107

(41) This is quite delicious. ············ 109

(42) Could I have some more, please? ············ 111

(43) I've had enough, thank you. ············ 113

Specific Vocabulary of Cooking ············ 114

VII Association

(44) Hello. ············ 117

(45) Please. Thank you. ············ 119

(46) *Itadakimasu.* (Bon appétit!/Enjoy your food!) ············ 121

(47) I have had enough, thank you. ············ 123

(48) *Wā, ureshii*! (Oh, I am pleased!/That's great!) ············ 125

(49) *Ojama shimashita.* (Thank you very much./I am afraid I've taken up too much of your time.) ············ 127

(50) Take care of yourselves. ············ 129

Family names and given names of Japanese ············ 130

VIII Getting to know Japan

(51) I went to see *Kabuki.* ············ 133

(52) Japan is a beautiful country, isn't it? ············ 135

(53) Congratulations. ············ 137

(4) Not very much. ············ 139

(55) *Ā bikkuri shita.* (You gave me such a surprise!) ············ 141

(56) Really sweet. ············ 143

(57) Why? ············ 145

(58) Then, what will happen next? ············ 147

Japanese Holidays ············ 148

第9章　トラブル

（59）あれー，どうしよう。……150
（60）ここが痛いんです。……152
（61）だれか，助けて。……154
（62）熱があります。……156
（63）いつできますか。……158
（64）助けて。痛いよう。……160
（65）とってもこわかった。……162
（66）ビザの書きかえです。……164
（67）電車に乗り遅れました。……166
病院……168

第10章　便利な表現

（68）うそー，ほんと。……170
（69）わかんない。……172
（70）あれ，やだ。……174
（71）こんなにたくさん。……176
（72）それは残念。……178
（73）あー，せいせいした。……180
（74）さっぱりした。……182
体の部分名称……184
色／日本の年中行事……185
地名クイズ……186
カタカナクイズ……187
日本の家庭料理の作り方(1)……188
日本の家庭料理の作り方(2)……190
日本語化した英語……192

IX Troubles

(59) Oh, what am I going to do? ……151
(60) I have a pain here. ……153
(61) Help! Somebody. ……155
(62) I've got a temperature. ……157
(63) When will it be ready? ……159
(64) Help! I've been hurt. ……161
(65) I was so frightened. ……163
(66) To renew my visa. ……165
(67) I missed the train. ……167
The hospital ……168

X Convenient expressions

(68) I can't believe it! ……171
(69) I don't know. ……173
(70) Oh, no! ……175
(71) That's a lot! ……177
(72) That's a pity! ……179
(73) Oh, I'm so relieved. ……181
(74) I feel refreshed. ……183
Parts of the human body ……184
Colors／Annual events in each of the four seasons ……185
Map Quiz ……186
Katakana Quiz ……187
Recipes for cooking Japanese dishes at home. (1) ……189
Recipes for cooking Japanese dishes at home. (2) ……191
Japlish ……192

コラム

日本人ははずかしがり屋 ……18
一日のあいさつ ……20
返事のしかたに注意 ……22
今日の天気がはじめのあいさつ ……24
あやまりかた ……26
日本人の中に入っていこう ……28
「いろいろ」は「いろいろ」です ……30
日本で住居を探すのはたいへん 34
部屋探しの条件は異なる ……36
住居のいろいろ ……38
住居が決ってから ……40
サインと印鑑（はんこ） ……42
日本の教育制度 ……44
外国人お断りの理由 ……46
近所づきあい ……48
求職と求人広告 ……52
第一印象が大事 ……54
日本で暮らすなら日本語を学ぼう 56
日本語学校について ……58
異国で働くには我慢が必要 ……60
コミュニケーションは具体的な表現で ……62
まじめな社員は職場の宝 ……64
日本人が就職するのもたいへん 66
ワリカンでやきとり屋へ ……68
目上の人にはていねいに ……72
留守宅配達の宅配便・書留郵便 ……74
日用必需品の買いかた ……76
公衆電話のかけかた ……78
国際電話のかけかた ……80
教会と礼拝について ……82
美容院と理髪店 ……84
お礼をくり返す日本人 ……86
まず路線図を手に入れよう ……90
乗車券の買いかた ……92
バスの利用のしかた ……94
旅行代理店を利用しよう ……96
専門店の買い物を楽しもう ……100
日本のデパートのサービスは超一流 ……102
ディスカウントショップを探そう ……104
外国人のための情報誌 ……106

Column

Japanese are often shy with strangers. · 19

Greeting during the course of the day. · 21

It is important to understand the Japanese way of answering questions. · 23

Talking about the weather is an "icebreaker". · · · · · · · · · · · · · · · · · · 25

How to apologize. · · · · · · · · · · · · · 27

Get into Japanese. · · · · · · · · · · · · · · 29

"*Iroiro*" means "*Iroiro*". · · · · · · · · 31

It is very difficult to find a place to live. · 35

There are many different conditions for room hunting. · · · · · · · · · · · · · · 37

Various possibilities · · · · · · · · · · · ·39

After you have settled in. · · · · · · · · 41

Sign and 'Hanko' (Seal) · · · · · · · · · 43

The education system in Japan · · · ·45

The reasons why it is difficult for foreigners to find a room. · · · · · · · · 47

Associating with your neighbors · · ·49

Job hunting and a "help wanted" advertisement · · · · · · · · · · · · · · · · ·53

First impressions are very important. · 55

Now that you are living in Japan why not study the Japanese language? · · 57

About Japanese language schools · ·59

You have to be patient when you work in Japan. · 61

Communication should be held in a tangible way. · · · · · · · · · · · · · · · · · 63

An earnest employee is a treasure at work. · 65

It is hard to find employment, even for the Japanese. · · · · · · · · · · · · · · · · · · 67

Going Dutch at a yakitori bar · · · ·69

Be polite to elderly people. · · · · · · 73

Special delivery and registered mail came while you were out. · · · · · · · · 75

How to buy daily necessities. · · · · · 77

How to use a public telephone. · · · 79

How to make an international telephone call. · · · · · · · · · · · · · · · · 81

Churches and services · · · · · · · · · ·83

Hairdresser and barber shop · · · · ·85

The Japanese repeatedly express their gratitude. · 87

First of all get a transport map. · · · 91

How to buy a ticket. · · · · · · · · · · · · 93

How to use a bus. · · · · · · · · · · · · · · 95

Make use of travel agency. · · · · · · · 97

Enjoy shopping at specialty shop. 101

国際色豊かな日本の食事 ····108
何でもトライしてみませんか ··110
日本の飲み物いろいろ ········112
日本の家庭を訪問してみたい ··116
「どうぞ」「どうも」で十分通じます ····118
「いただきます」「ごちそうさま」120
「もう，けっこうです」は便利なことば ··122
町内会の人とつきあおう ·····124
日本人の移動の時期 ··········126
ホームステイができれば最高 ··128
日本特有の民衆劇・歌舞伎 ···132
四季を通して雨量が多い ····134
もしも結婚式に招待されたら ·136
日本の「わび」と「さび」····138
日本の葬式とお墓 ············140
テレビ番組 ····················142
日本のビジネスマンの生活 ····144
人気がある日本の武道 ········146
電車・バス・タクシーの忘れ物 ·150
具合の悪い個所は手で示す ····152
犯罪に遭ったとき ············154
いろいろな症状の伝えかた ···156
機械・機器の修理 ············158
交通事故には十分注意を ····160
広域避難場所 ················162
出入国管理法を守ろう ······164
引っ越しするときは ··········166
四季と１２か月 ··············170
疑問の表現 ··················172
曜日と日時 ··················174
反対語 ······················176
なぜそんなことば知ってるの(1) ·178
なぜそんなことば知ってるの(2) ·180
なぜそんなことば知ってるの(3) ·182

Service in a Japanese department store is first-rate. ·················103

Find out about discount shops. ···105

Information magazines for foreigners. ···························107

Meals in Japan can be very international ·················109

Why don't you try everything? ···111

Beverages in Japan ···········113

Visiting a Japanese family is desirable. ···························117

"*Dōzo*", "*Dōmo*" is enough to communicate your thanks. ······ 119

"*Itadakimasu*", "*Gochisōsama*" ·· 121

"*Mō kekkō desu.*" is a convenient phrase. ····················· 123

Associate with the people living in the same neighborhood. ··········· 125

The periods when Japanese people take a trip ····················127

Your best opportunity might be when you can experience a homestay. ·· 129

Kabuki: Japanese popular traditional theater performance. ············ 133

There is a lot of rain throughout the four seasons. ················· 135

You may be invited to a wedding ceremony. ···················· 137

Japan's '*Wabi*', and '*Sabi*' ······ 139

Japanese funerals and graves ····141

TV Programs ················143

The life of a Japanese businessman145

The popular Japnaese martial arts ·147

Lost property in the train, bus and taxi ···························151

Indicate the spot where you feel sick or pain with your hand. ··········· 153

When you experience trouble. ··· 155

How to describe various symptoms. ·· ························· 157

Repairing machines and instruments. · ························· 159

Be careful to avoid traffic accidents. · ························· 161

Evacuation areas ·············163

Observe the immigration laws! ·· 165

When you move house. ········ 167

Four seasons and 12 months ·····171

The expression of questions ·····173

Days and times ··············175

Antonyms ··················177

How did you come to know these expressions?(1) ··············· 179

How did you come to know these expressions?(2) ··············181

How did you come to know these expressions?(3) ··············· 183

ローマ字表　The Roman Alphabet

のばす音は，母音（a, i, u, e, o）のうえに ¯ をつけて表します。

A long-held note is indicate with a ¯ above the vowel (a, i, u, e, o).

例）かあ，カー　→　kā

あ	い	う	え	お	わ		を	が	ぎ	ぐ	げ	ご
ア	イ	ウ	エ	オ	ワ		ヲ	ガ	ギ	グ	ゲ	ゴ
a	**i**	**u**	**e**	**o**	**wa**		**o**	**ga**	**gi**	**gu**	**ge**	**go**
か	き	く	け	こ	ん			ざ	じ	ず	ぜ	ぞ
カ	キ	ク	ケ	コ	ン			ザ	ジ	ズ	ゼ	ゾ
ka	**ki**	**ku**	**ke**	**ko**	**n**			**za**	**ji**	**zu**	**ze**	**zo**
さ	し	す	せ	そ	きゃ	きゅ	きょ	だ	ぢ	づ	で	ど
サ	シ	ス	セ	ソ	キャ	キュ	キョ	ダ	ヂ	ヅ	デ	ド
sa	**shi**	**su**	**se**	**so**	**kya**	**kyu**	**kyo**	**da**	**ji**	**zu**	**de**	**do**
た	ち	つ	て	と	しゃ	しゅ	しょ	ば	び	ぶ	べ	ぼ
タ	チ	ツ	テ	ト	シャ	シュ	ショ	バ	ビ	ブ	ベ	ボ
ta	**chi**	**tsu**	**te**	**to**	**sha**	**shu**	**sho**	**ba**	**bi**	**bu**	**be**	**bo**
な	に	ぬ	ね	の	ちゃ	ちゅ	ちょ	ぱ	ぴ	ぷ	ぺ	ぽ
ナ	ニ	ヌ	ネ	ノ	チャ	チュ	チョ	パ	ピ	プ	ペ	ポ
na	**ni**	**nu**	**ne**	**no**	**cha**	**chu**	**cho**	**pa**	**pi**	**pu**	**pe**	**po**
は	ひ	ふ	へ	ほ	にゃ	にゅ	にょ	ぎゃ		ぎゅ		ぎょ
ハ	ヒ	フ	ヘ	ホ	ニャ	ニュ	ニョ	ギャ		ギュ		ギョ
ha	**hi**	**fu**	**he**	**ho**	**nya**	**nyu**	**nyo**	**gya**		**gyu**		**gyo**
ま	み	む	め	も	ひゃ	ひゅ	ひょ	じゃ		じゅ		じょ
マ	ミ	ム	メ	モ	ヒャ	ヒュ	ヒョ	ジャ		ジュ		ジョ
ma	**mi**	**mu**	**me**	**mo**	**hya**	**hyu**	**hyo**	**ja**		**ju**		**jo**
や		ゆ		よ	みゃ	みゅ	みょ	びゃ		びゅ		びょ
ヤ		ユ		ヨ	ミャ	ミュ	ミョ	ビャ		ビュ		ビョ
ya		**yu**		**yo**	**mya**	**myu**	**myo**	**bya**		**byu**		**byo**
ら	り	る	れ	ろ	りゃ	りゅ	りょ	ぴゃ		ぴゅ		ぴょ
ラ	リ	ル	レ	ロ	リャ	リュ	リョ	ピャ		ピュ		ピョ
ra	**ri**	**ru**	**re**	**ro**	**rya**	**ryu**	**ryo**	**pya**		**pyu**		**pyo**

I

あいさつ
Greeting

はじめまして。

Hajimemashite.

「はじめまして」という初対面のあいさつは，そのまま英語には訳せません。

ダイアローグ

F　はじめまして。ロジャー・ブラウンです。
　　Hajimemashite.　Rojā·Buraun desu.

J　わたしは小川です。
　　Watashi wa Ogawa desu.

F　どうぞよろしく。
　　Dōzo yoroshiku.

J　こちらこそよろしく，ブラウンさん。
　　Kochira koso yoroshiku, Buraun -san.

日本人ははずかしがり屋

外国人とのつきあいになれている日本人でしたら，初対面のときから自然に会話が進みますが，たいていの日本人は，外国人にたいしてはずかしがり屋です。

外国人から握手を求められて，やっと手を出します。ふつう日本人同士では握手をしません。おじぎをするのが礼儀だからです。なかには相手の目を見ずに下をむいている人がいます。はずかしいのと，外国語でペラペラ話されて，わからなかったら困るからです。決して，外国人がきらいなのではありません。そんな日本人に出会ったら，ちょっと日本語で話しかけてみませんか。すぐに心がうちとけて笑顔が返ってきますよ。

How do you do?

'Hajimemashite', used when being introduced for the first time, is difficult to translate literally.

Dialog

F **How do you do? I'm Roger Brown.**

J **I'm Ogawa.**

F **Nice to meet you.**

J **Nice to meet you, too, Mr. Brown.**

Japanese are often shy with strangers.

If a Japanese is accustomed to associating with foreigners, he will have no problem carrying on a natural conversation. However, most Japanese are shy among foreigners.

When a foreigner offers his hand, some Japanese will shake hands awkwardly while bowing at the same time. Handshaking is not a common practice among the Japanese. When they greet each other, they bow. When shaking hands, some Japanese will look downward, avoiding eye contact. This attitude comes from their shyness, as well as from the embarrassment they might feel if they are spoken to in English.

However, it does not mean that they dislike foreigners. If you happen to meet such a Japanese, why don't you try to speak in Japanese? They will open their hearts at once and smile back at you.

こんにちは。

Kon-nichi-wa.

ふつう昼間にかわすあいさつです。

ダイアローグ

F　洋子さん，こんにちは。
　　Yōko-san, kon-nichi-wa.

J　こんにちは，メアリー。
　　Kon-nichi-wa, Meari.

F　お元気ですか。
　　Ogenki desu ka?

J　ええ，おかげさまで。
　　Ee, okagesama de.

一日のあいさつ

朝起きてからお昼までは「おはようございます」，昼から夕方までは「こんにちは」，日が落ちて暗くなったら「こんばんは」，そして寝る前のあいさつは「おやすみなさい」と言います。

また，相手の体調などをたずねる場合，「元気」に「お」をつけて，ていねいに言いますが，それに答えて自分は元気だと言うときは「お」はつけません。

「おかげさまで」という慣用句も，日本人がよく使う言い回しです。まわりの人たちのいろいろな助けがあって自分が生きている，という日本人が共通して持っている気持ちを，さらにていねいに「さま」をつけて表しています。

Konnichiwa. (Hello.)

Usually 'Konnichiwa' is used in the daytime.

Dialog

F	**Hello, Yōko.**
J	**Hello, Mary.**
F	**How are you?**
J	**Very well, thank you.**

Greeting during the course of the day

From morning till noon, we use '*Ohayōgozaimasu*', from noon to evening, '*Konnichiwa*', after dark, '*Konbanwa*', and before retiring, '*Oyasuminasai*'.

Also, when Japanese ask about other people's health they use the polite form '*o*' with 'Genki', but when answering that question they don't use '*o*' for ourselves.

'*Okagesamade*' is often used among Japanese people. It expresses a characteristic Japanese feeling that they all exist by virtue of help from their neighbors and they use '*sama*' to show respect.

はい［ええ］。いいえ。

Hai [Ee]. Iie.

肯定と否定の言いかたです。

ダイアローグ

J　ジョンソンさんですか。
　Jonson-san desu ka?

F　はい，そうです。
　Hai, sō desu.

J　トーマス・ジョンソンさんですね。
　Tōmasu･Jonson desu ne?

F　いいえ，デビッド・ジョンソンです。
　Iie, Debiddo･Jonson desu.

返事のしかたに注意

日本語の「はい」「いいえ」は，肯定否定文に対する答えとしては簡単ですが，否定疑問文に対する答えの場合，気をつけなくてはいけません。英語では，質問の答えが「イエス」なら，肯定疑問文で聞かれても否定疑問文で聞かれても，答えはあくまでも「イエス」です。たとえば「あなたは明日会社へは来られませんね」という否定疑問文に対して，日本人は「はい」と答えます。その意味合いは「はい，あなたのいう通り，私は来られません」ということです。いっぽう，英語の答えは「いいえ，私は来られません」となり，来社できない否定的な事実に対応します。気をつけてください。

Hai. (Yes). *Iie*. (No).

Negative and affirmative expressions.

Dialog

J **Are you Mr. Johnson?**

F **Yes, I am.**

J **You are Thomas Johnson, aren't you?**

F **No, I'm David Johnson.**

It is important to understand the Japanese way ofanswering questions.

The Japanese use of "Yes" and "No" is the same as in English for simple, affirmative questions. However, there is a difference when it comes to negative questions. A negative question such as "You can't come to the office tomorrow, can you?" is answered "Yes" by a Japanese; the logic being, "Yes, you are right, I can't come." The English answer will be "No, I can't.", as they respond to the negative idea of not being able to come. So, be careful.

もういちど。すみません。

Mōichido. Sumi masen.

聞きとれなかったときに言います。

ダイアローグ

J　ひさしぶりのお天気ですね。
Hisashiburi no otenki desu ne.

F　え？もういちど。すみません。
E? Mōichido. Sumi masen.

J　あー，今日はいいお天気ですね。
Ah, kyōwa ii otenki desu ne.

F　ええ，ほんとに。
Ee, honto ni.

今日の天気がはじめのあいさつ

ちょっと言葉をかわすとき，「今日は暑いですね」「ほんとうに寒いですね」「蒸しますね」「いやな天気ですね」「雨ばかり降って，いやですね」など天気を話題にすることがよくあります。

道で会ったとき，日本人が何気なくかわすあいさつに「どちらへお出かけですか」があります。答えかたは「ええ，ちょっとそこまで」というように，あいまいなことが多いものです。完全な回答になっていなくても，それがお互いのあいさつなのです。このようなむだな会話にも人と人とのつきあいの大事な部分が含まれています。

お天気のあいさつには「ええ，ほんとうに」，「どちらへ」に対しては「ええ，ちょっと（買い物に，東京へ，旅行に，……）」と答えればいいのです。

Could you say that again?

You can use this when you can't hear what the other person says.

Dialog

J **We haven't had such a nice day for a long time.**

F **Sorry? Could you say that again, please?**

J **Well, it's a nice day today.**

F **Yes, indeed.**

Talking about the weather is an "icebreaker".

When Japanese exchange greetings, they often talk about the weather. For example, "Today is hot, isn't it?", "It's really cold.", "It's humid.", "It's nasty weather.", "It's been raining all day. Horrible, isn't it?"

When Japanese meet acquaintances in the street, they will greet them casually. "Where are you going?" Answers for this question are usually vague, like "Well, just around the corner." This is not a complete answer but there may be a good reason for this kind of answer.

You can answer the weather questions with "*Ee, Hontō ni*," and the question about where you are going you can answer like "*Ee, chotto* . . ." (shopping, to Tokyo, or travel to . . .)

しつれいします。

Shitsurei shimasu.

家や部屋のなかに案内されたときに言います。

ダイアローグ

J　こちらへどうぞ。
Kochirae　dōzo.

F　しつれいします。
Shitsurei　shimasu.

J　あっ，くつをぬいで。
A,　kutsu o nuide.

F　ごめんなさい。
Gomen-nasai.

あやまりかた

日本は人口過密ですから，街でも電車でもよく足を踏まれたりぶつかったりします。「ごめんなさい」が一般的なあやまりかたです。「失礼」といって軽く頭をさげるのは軽いあやまりかたです。「あっ，どうも，すみません」はとっさのときのあやまりかたですが，かなり日本語に慣れていないと言えないでしょう。

「しつれいします」の「しつれい」は，日本語特有のニュアンスで，あやまる意味とは異なります。

「どうもすみません」も一般的なあやまりかたですが，「すみませんが」とか「ちょっと，すみません」は何かたずねるときの言いかたです。

Excuse me. (Thank you.)

Japanese use these when they are ushered into a house or a room.

Dialog

J **This way, please.**

F **Thank you.**

J **Oh, take off your shoes, please.**

F **Sorry.**

How to apologize.

Japanese often step on other people's feet or bump into other people on the street and in the train, because they have a high population density. "*Gomennasai* " is a common expression to apologize. Saying "*Shitsurei* " with a light bow is a casual way to apologize. "*A, dōmo sumimasen*" is an apology which is said reflectively by a person who wants to say something like "Sorry about that!". The correct intonation of the words is rather special, so it is best to use it only after you become thoroughly familiar with the Japanese language.

"*Shitsurei* " of "*Shitsureishimasu*" is a characteristic nuance of Japanese which is somewhat different from apologizing.

"*Dōmo sumimasen*" is a common expression of apology. Japanese use "*Sumimasenga,*", and "*Chotto sumimasen*" when they ask for something.

ありがとうございます。

Arigatō gozaimasu.

お礼，感謝を表すていねいな言いかたです。

ダイアローグ

J　コーヒー，いかがですか。
Kō hi, ikaga desu ka?

F　ありがとうございます。
Arigatō gozaimasu.

J　ミルク，入いれますか。
Miruku, iremasu ka?

F　お願いします。
Onegai shimasu.

日本人の中に入っていこう

日本人は，いったんうちとけると，とても親切です。そして，あなたのお国のことをいろいろ知りたがります。あなたも積極的に日本を知ろうと心がけてください。

日本語は難しい言語といわれていますが，本書ではもっとも日常的でやさしい日本語をとりあげました。

はやく日本に溶けこむには，いつも外国人同士でいないで，少しずつ日本語を使って日本人の中に入っていきましょう。

Thank you very much.

The polite way to express acknowledgment and gratitude.

Dialog

J **Would you like a cup of coffee?**

F **Thank you very much.**

J **Do you want some milk?**

F **Yes, please.**

Get into Japanese.

Japanese people can be very kind, once they get to know you. Also, they are interested in learning about your own country. So in return, please be enthusiastic about learning things about Japan.

It is said that Japanese is a particularly difficult language to learn, though in this book we have tried to use the most simple and natural, but correct, Japanese. Don't always "hang out" with friends from your own country, but try to mix with the Japanese and use their language, so that little by little you will get to know both the Japanese language and the Japanese people themselves.

さようなら。

Sayōnara.

別(わか)れるときのあいさつです。

ダイアローグ

J　今日(きょう)はとても楽(たの)しかった。
Kyō wa totemo tanoshikatta.

F　いろいろありがとうございました。
Iroiro arigatō gozaimashita.

J　どういたしまして。
Dō itashimashite.

F　ではまた。さようなら。
Dewa mata. Sayōnara.

「いろいろ」は「いろいろ」です

日本人はあまり具体的(ぐたいてき)な表現(ひょうげん)をしません。だまっていても心に思(おも)うことがお互(たが)いに通(つう)じあうことを大切(たいせつ)にするからです。これを以心伝心(いしんでんしん)といいます。

そのひとつの例(れい)が「いろいろ」です。知人(ちじん)の家(いえ)を訪問(ほうもん)して，ごちそうになったり，話(はなし)を聞(き)いたり，帰(かえ)りにおみやげをもらったり，これらをひっくるめて「いろいろありがとうございました」といいます。

「いろいろすみません」という言いかたは，ちょっとした親切(しんせつ)をいくつか受(う)けたときに使(つか)います。

若(わか)い人同士(どうし)の「さようなら」は「バイバイ」とか「じゃあね」と言うこともあります。

Good-bye.

Said on parting company.

Dialog

J **I had a very exciting day.**

F **Thank you very much for everything.**

J **Not at all.**

F **See you again. Good-bye.**

"Iroiro" means "Iroiro".

Japanese people consider that they are communicating at the best level when they come to a state of understanding each other without having to use many words. There is a proverb : "*I shin denshin*" in Japanese, which means that if two people develop a very close relationship, they can each sense what the other is thinking.

After having had dinner, conversation and receiving a small gift from a friend at his or her house, they say "*Iroiro arigatō gozaimashita*", combining all the kind actions into one.

Japanese use "*Iroiro sumimasen.*" when they receive some small kindness. Between young people, they sometimes use "bye-bye" or "*Jāne*".

あなたの「干支(えと)」は何(なん)ですか？

（十二支(じゅうにし) the twelve signs）			（生(う)まれ年(どし) the year of birth 19-）				
子（ね）	ねずみ	鼠 Mouse	'96	'84	'72	'60	'48
丑（うし）	うし	牛 Ox	'97	'85	'73	'61	'49
寅（とら）	とら	虎 Tiger	'98	'86	'74	'62	'50
卯（う）	うさぎ	兎 Rabbit	'99	'87	'75	'63	'51
辰（たつ）	たつ	竜 Dragon	'88	'76	'64	'52	'40
巳（み）	へび	蛇 Snake	'89	'77	'65	'53	'41
午（うま）	うま	馬 Horse	'90	'78	'66	'54	'42
未（ひつじ）	ひつじ	羊 Sheep	'91	'79	'67	'55	'43
申（さる）	さる	猿 Monkey	'92	'80	'68	'56	'44
酉（とり）	にわとり	鶏 Cock	'93	'81	'69	'57	'45
戌（いぬ）	いぬ	犬 Dog	'94	'82	'70	'58	'46
亥（い）	いのしし	猪 Wild Eschwein	'95	'83	'71	'59	'47

II

住まいを定める
Settling down

駅はどこですか。

Eki wa doko desuka?

「どこですか」は場所を聞くときの言いかたです。

ダイアローグ

F　駅はどこですか。
Eki wa doko desuka.

J　こっちの道をまっすぐ。じきですよ。
Kocchino michi o massugu. Jikidesu yo.

F　不動産屋さんを探しています。
Fudōsan-ya-san o sagashite imasu.

J　駅のそばにたくさんありますよ。
Ekino soba ni takusan arimasu yo.

日本で住居を探すのはたいへん

日本へ来きたら，住むところを探さなければなりません。まず自分の国から来ている友人を訪ねてみましょう。そして情報集めをしてから部屋探しをするとよいでしょう。いちばんはやいのは不動産屋へ行くことです。聞くだけならお金はかかりません。

しかし，住居が決まるまで当面の住いが必要です。といってホテルに何日もいたらお金がたいへんです。

日本には敷金・保証金・礼金・前家賃などの制度があり，生活様式の異なる外国人には貸したがらないという問題があります。ただ，外国人の事情を理解し，電気・ガス・水道・電話とりつけの手続きまでしてくれたり，敷金・礼金をとらない不動産屋や大家さんもいますので，根気よく探してみましょう。

Where is the station?

"Dokodesuka" is an expression used to ask about places.

Dialog

F **Where is the station?**

J **Straight ahead. It's not far.**

F **I'm looking for a real estate agency.**

J **Yes. There are a lot around the station.**

It is very difficult to find a place to live.

You must find a place to live when you come to Japan. First of all, why don't you contact friends from your own country? After getting information from them, you will be better able to start looking for your own place. The quickest way is to go to a real estate agency. It doesn't cost anything to make an inquiry.

But you need somewhere to stay until you find your place. Hotels are expensive.

In Japan, they have system in which the prospective renter has to pay "key" money as a deposit, guarantee money, and thank-you money to the real estate agency, as well as the first month's rent in advance. Many landlords don't want to rent rooms to foreigners because they may have different habits and standards of living. Still, there are some landlords who understand the foreigner's situation and they are kind enough to help with the procedures necessary to have the electricity, gas, water and telephone put on, on behalf of foreign people. Or some may not ask you for key money, so be patient.

アパートを探しています。

Apāto o sagashite imasu.

不動産屋に入って，すぐにいうことばです。

ダイアローグ

F　アパートを探しています。
　　Apāto o sagashite imasu.

J　駅から遠くてよかったらありますよ。
　　Eki kara tōkute yokattara arimasu yo.

F　見せてもらえますか。
　　Misete morae masu ka?

J　いいですよ。ちょっと待ってください。
　　Iidesu yo. Chotto matte kudasai.

部屋探しの条件は異なる

あなたの資格によって部屋探しの条件が違ってきます。

①留学生　国費留学生であれば，あらかじめ宿舎は用意されていますが，一般留学生は自分で部屋探しをしなければなりません。それには，日本人の保証人が必要です。学校の先生などに相談してみましょう。家賃が安いと，トイレ・風呂・台所は共同になります。

②外国語会話教師など　日本で外国語教師になりたいのなら，日本の企業もしくは英会話スクールがスポンサーになってくれることが条件です。そうすればアパート探しの保証も得られるでしょう。収入に応じ通勤便利な住居が探せます。

③労働者　雇用主の条件によって住むところはさまざまです。

I'm looking for an apartment house.

Use these words when you visit a real estate agency.

Dialog

F **I'm looking for an apartment house.**

J **We have one if you don't mind being some distance from the station.**

F **Can I have a look?**

J **Yes, you can. One moment, please.**

There are many different conditions for room hunting.

The condition for room hunting differs depending on your qualifications.

①**Students**: Students on government expense can have a room prepared for them, but private students have to find a room by themselves. In that case, you need a Japanese guarantor. When you need a guarantor, ask your school teachers. When the rent is cheap, you may have to share the toilet, bathroom or kitchen.

②**Language** teacher, etc: If you want to become a language teacher in Japan, the Japanese firm or language school you work for must be your sponsor for your work visa. And when hunting for a room, you can get a guaranty from the school for your room, also. You can find a room convenient for commuting to work according to your salary.

③**Laborer**: It depends on the agreement with your employer.

ここを貸してください。

Koko o kashite kudasai.

借りたい部屋が決まったらこう言います。

ダイアローグ

J　このアパートは新しいですよ。
Kono apāto wa atarashii desu yo.

F　でも，高いですね。
Demo, takai desu ne.

J　こっちはすこし安いですよ。
Kocchi wa sukoshi yasui desu yo.

F　ここを貸してください。
Koko o kashite kudasai.

住居のいろいろ

■一戸建て住宅　独立して建てられた家。日本人でもなかなか手に入らない。

■マンション　高級アパート。高価で買い取りが多い。

■公団住宅　入居する人の国籍は問わないが，公開抽選で倍率はたいへん高い。

■会社社員寮　企業が社員のために持っている住宅。家賃は格安。

■学生寮　一定の資格をもった留学生が共同で生活する施設です。

■下宿　家主の一部屋を借り，食事付きの場合もある。

■ユースホステル　予約がとれれば，3日以内なら宿泊できる。臨時には格安。

■ウィークリー・マンション　週単位・月単位の契約で必要家具付き。しかし，割高。

■アパート　ピンからキリまで価格次第。トイレ・シャワー付きから共同までいろいろある。予算に応じてアパートがいちばん無難。

I'd like to rent this room.

Say these words to the agency when you have decided on the room.

Dialog

J **This apartment is newly built.**

F **But it's expensive, isn't it?**

J **This one is a bit cheaper.**

F **I'd like to rent this room.**

Various possibilities

・Houses: Built as an independent house. Even the Japanese can't readily afford them.

・ Apartment houses: High-class apartments. They are expensive and usually for purchase rather than renting.

・ Housing corporation's apartment houses: A person of any nationality can be a tenant, but you have to be part of an open lottery, which is very competitive.

・ Company dormitories: Companies have apartments for employees. Rent is quite cheap.

・ Student dormitories: Students who have a certain qualification live together in these facilities.

・ Lodgings: Renting a room from the landlords' house. It sometimes includes meals.

・ Youth hostels: It is possible to stay for 3 nights if you can book a room. Cheap for a temporary stay.

・ Weekly apartment house: This is let on a weekly or monthly basis. Furnished, but comparatively expensive.

・ Apartment houses: They vary according to the rent. There are rooms with toilet and shower, or you may have to share those facilities. Apartment houses with a reasonable rent are most suitable for foreigners.

外国人登録にきました。

Gaikokujin-tōroku ni kimashita.

市［区］役所で手続きをするときに言います。

ダイアローグ

F　外国人登録にきました。
Gaikokujin-tōroku ni kimashita.

J　市民課へ行ってください。
Shimin-ka e itte kudasai.

F　それはどこですか。
Sore wa doko desu ka?

J　１番のカウンターです。
Ichiban no kauntā desu.

住居が決まってから

①外国人登録　日本に９０日以上住むときは入国後９０日以内に市［区］役所で外国人登録の手続きをしなければなりません。パスポートと写真２枚（3.5cm×4.5cm）が必要です。作成には２週間くらいかかります。

②国民健康保険　これも市［区］役所で手続きができます。

③電気・ガス・水道　引っ越しの日に来てもらうように手配しておきます。不動産屋に聞けば教えてくれます。

④電話　事前に１１６番にかけて，引っ越しの日に来てもらいましょう。

⑤郵便局　住民になったことを通知しておきます。

⑥表札　入口か郵便受けに名前を明示しておきましょう。

⑦近所あいさつ　向う三軒両隣りには必ずあいさつしましょう。

I've come to register as a foreign resident.

Say these words, when you register as an alien at the ward office counter.

Dialog

F **I've come to register as a foreign resident.**

J **Please go to the citizen's section.**

F **Where is it?**

J **It's in the counter No. 1.**

After you have settled in.

① Foreign Registration: When you intend to stay in Japan for more than 90 days, you have to register at your municipal or ward office within 14 days of your arrival. You need your passport and two photos (3cm×4cm). The process takes about 2 weeks.

② National Health Insurance: You can become insured at your municipal or ward office.

③ Electricity・Gas・Water Service: You have to arrange for them on the day you move in. Real estate agencies can tell you how to do it.

④ Telephone: Call 116 and ask an engineer to come on the day.

⑤ Post Office: Give notice of your address to the nearest Post Office.

⑥ Name plate: Put your name plate on the door or the letter box.

⑦ Neighbors: Introduce yourself to the neighbors.

初めて来ました。

Hajimete kimashita.

銀行・市役所などで，初めて来たことを窓口で伝えることばです。

ダイアローグ

F　初めて来ました。
Hajimete kimashita.

J　ご新規のお取り引きですね。
Goshinki no otorihiki desu ne.

F　1,000円だけ入れます。
Sen-en dake ire masu.

J　この用紙に記入してください。
Kono yōshi ni kinyū shite kudasai.

サインと印鑑（はんこ）

日本で生活すると，印鑑を使う機会がよくあります。市［区］役所や銀行で申請する用紙には必ず印鑑を押す欄があります。また配達物の受け取りの証明として印鑑を求められることがあります。

さらに銀行ローンの契約や会社設立などには実印（市役所に登録した印鑑）が必要です。これはふつうの印鑑（はんこ）とは違う大事なものです。

外国ではすべてサインで処理します。最近は日本でもほとんどサインで済むようになってきましたが，日本に定住しようとする外国人は自分の名前をカタカナか漢字で刻んだ印鑑を持っているほうが便利です。

This is my first time to come here.

These words will help the teller to understand that you haven't been to a bank in Japan before.

Dialog

F This is my first time to come here.

J You would like to open an account, wouldn't you?

F I'd like to start with 1,000 yen.

J Would you fill in this form, please?

Sign and 'Hanko' (Seal)

When it comes to living in Japan, you'll often have opportunities to use a 'Hanko'. There are always spaces for 'Hanko' on the application forms at the municipal (ward) office or at banks. Sometimes you need a 'Hanko' for proof of having received deliveries.

Besides the hanko, you need a 'Jitsuin' (a registered seal at the municipal office) when you make a contract for a bank loan or establish a company. This 'Jitsuin' is different from the ordinary hanko and is quite an important thing.

Recently, it has become possible to use signatures instead of a 'Hanko' because most foreigners use signatures. But if you intend on staying in Japan for a long time, it will be covenient to have your own 'Hanko' written in Katakana or Kanji.

こどもの学校のことで来ました。

Kodomo no gakkō no kotode kimashita.

市役所でこどもの学校の相談に来たことを伝えるときに言います。

ダイアローグ

F　こどもの学校のことで来ました。
Kodomo no gakkō no koto de kimashita.

J　学務課へ行ってください。
Gakumu-ka e itte kudasai.

F　それはなんですか。
Sore wa nan desu ka?

J　10番の窓口で聞いてください。
Jū-ban no madoguchi de kiite kudasai.

日本の教育制度

日本の義務教育は小学校の6年間と中学校の3年間です。小学校入学以前の幼児は保育所か幼稚園へ行きます。中学を終えるとふつう，高等学校へ3年間通います。その後は短期大学もしくは大学に進む人もいます。日本では4月に新学期が始まり，翌年3月で1学年が終わります。小・中学校は住んでいる場所で学校が決まります。授業料と教科書は無料です。授業はすべて日本語です。インターナショナル・スクールは東京や横浜などの大都市以外でみつけるのは難しいでしょう。

保育所の申し込みは市の児童課へ，幼稚園に入れたい場合は直接幼稚園にいって申し込んでください。

I've come to inquire about a school for my child.

These words are said when you want to inquire about the Japanese education system at the municipal office, because you want to send your child to a local Japanese school.

Dialog

F **I've come to inquire about a school for my child.**

J **Please go to the educational affairs section.**

F **What is it?**

J **Ask at the counter No. 10.**

The education system in Japan

Six years in primary school and three years in junior high school are compulsory for Japanese children. Befor eprimary school, there is nursery school and kindergarten. After finishing junior high school, most children go to high school for three years. After that, some people go to junior college or university. Terms begin in April and end in March. Which primary shool and which junior high school you go to will depend on your address. Tuition and textbooks are free. All the lessons in Japanese state schools are taught in Japanese. It might be difficult to find an international school outside of big cities like Tokyo or Yokohama.

When you wish to apply for a nursery school, you should go to the children's section of the municipal office. When you want your child to enter a kindergarten, you go to the kindergarten yourself and apply.

ゴミの日はいつですか。

Gomi no hi wa itsu desu ka?

ゴミを出だす日をたずねるときに言います。

ダイアローグ

F　ゴミの日はいつですか。
Gomi no hi wa itsu desu ka?

J　ここに書いてあります。
Kokoni kaite arimasu.

F　これは今日出してもいいですか。
Korewa kyō dashitemo iidesu ka?

J　缶は第1と第3火曜日です。
Kan wa daiichi to daisan kayōbi desu.

外国人お断りの理由

毎日の生活でゴミがでます。外国人に部屋を貸したがらない理由のひとつに，ゴミを分類しないでだす外国人が多いことをあげています。

ゴミをだす場所に英語の表示がないためわからないこともありますが，近所の人に聞いて，そのメモをカレンダーのわきにはっておいてください。ゴミの分類と収集日は地区によって異なりますが，だいたい次のように分けることが多いようです。

①普通ゴミ　台所からでる生ゴミや紙くず，布など　週3回

②分別ゴミ　1）金属類：缶・鍋など。乾電池はべつにして透明袋へ。
2）非金属類：ビン・ガラス・プラスチック類など。
分別ゴミは合わせて週1回。

③粗大ゴミ　テレビ・冷蔵庫・家具・マットレス・自転車などは，市の清掃事務所に連絡して取りにきてもらう。引っ越し時に出るゴミは，早目に連絡が必要。有料。

Which day should I put out the garbage/trash?

These words are said when you want to ask which day is a garbage collection day.

Dialog

F **Which day should I put out the garbage?**

J **It's written here.**

F **May I put it out today?**

J **You can put out empty cans on the first and third Tuesday.**

The reasons why it is difficult for foreigners to find a room.

Everyday life produces a lot of trash. One of the reasons why landlords won't rent rooms to foreigners is because they don't sort their garbage when they put it out.

Sometimes there are no English signs and you might not know which day is a trash clearance day. In that case, you can ask neighbors for the information and pin it up beside the calendar.

Classification and the collection day depends on the area, but usually in most cities the classification is as follows:

1) Garbage: garbage from the kitchen, papers, old clothes.
Collected three times a week.

2) Garbage to be separated: ① metals: cans, trash pans, etc. Batteries should be packed separately in a transparent bag.
② nonmetals: bottles, glass, plastic.
Collected once a week.

3) Bulky garbage: TV, refrigerators, furniture, mattresses, bicycles, etc. You have to request that the sanitation facility take these items away and pay for the service. It would be best for you to call the sanitation facility before you move from your place.

こんど越してきました。

Kondo koshite kimashita.

近所に引っ越しのあいさつをするときに言います。

ダイアローグ

F　こんど越してきました。
Kondo koshite kimashita.

J　ああ，そうですか。
Aa, sōdesu ka.

F　メアリーと申します。どうぞ，よろしく。
Meari to mōshi masu. Dōzo yoroshiku.

J　こちらこそ，よろしく。
Kochira koso yoroshiku.

近所づきあい

日本では新しい場所に引っ越したとき，となり近所に日本そばを配る習慣がありました。日本そばのそばと近所という意味のそばのごろ合わせです。いまでは名前を書いた小さな贈り物をもってあいさつにいくようです。同じアパートで毎日顔を合わせる人はもちろん，一軒家なら両隣りと向い側の3軒の家にはあいさつしておきましょう。いちどあいさつをかわすと何かと親切にしてくれます。

あいさつがないと，どこまでも関係ないと思われます。日常生活を楽しく送るためにも近所の人たちとよい関係を保つことが大切です。

I’ve moved in recently.

These words are said when you take a self-introduction to your neighbors.

Dialog

F **I’ve moved in recently.**

J **Oh, have you?**

F **My name is Mary. Nice to meet you.**

J **Nice to meet you, too.**

Associating with your neighbors

In Japan, there used to be a custom that when you moved into a new area, you offered Japanese noodles to your neighbors. The name for noodles (*soba*) sounds the same as the name for neighbors (*soba*) in Japanese, hence this choice of offering. Nowadays we introduce ourselves with a small gift, with our name written on it.

If you have moved into a house, you should call on your nearest neighbors. They may be the ones to look after you if you should need help.

Therefore, if you don’t introduce yourself they won’t recognize you as a neighbor. It is an important thing to have a good relationship with your neighbors in order to enjoy your life in Japan.

数え方（かぞえかた） Counting

				えんぴつ (Stift)	本（ほん） (Buch)	家（いえ） (Haus)
1・一	いち	one	ひとつ	いっぽん 1本	いっさつ 1冊	いっけん 1軒
2・二	に	two	ふたつ	にほん 2本	にさつ 2冊	にけん 2軒
3・三	さん	three	みっつ	さんぼん 3本	さんさつ 3冊	さんげん 3軒
4・四	し	four	よっつ	よんほん 4本	よんさつ 4冊	よんけん 4軒
5・五	ご	five	いつつ	ごほん 5本	ごさつ 5冊	ごけん 5軒
6・六	ろく	six	むっつ	ろっぽん 6本	ろくさつ 6冊	ろっけん 6軒
7・七	なな	seven	ななつ	ななほん 7本	ななさつ 7冊	ななけん 7軒
8・八	はち	eight	やっつ	はちほん 8本	はっさつ 8冊	はっけん 8軒
9・九	く	nine	ここのつ	きゅうほん 9本	きゅうさつ 9冊	きゅうけん 9軒
10・十	じゅう	ten	とう	じゅっぽん 10本	じゅっさつ 10冊	じゅっけん 10軒

人（ひと） (human-being)	物（もの） (fruit/box)	紙（かみ）・布（ぬの） (paper/cloth)	ごはん・わん (rice/soup)
ひとり 1人	いっこ 1個	いちまい 1枚	いっぱい 1杯
ふたり 2人	にこ 2個	にまい 2枚	にはい 2杯
さんにん 3人	さんこ 3個	さんまい 3枚	さんばい 3杯
よにん 4人	よんこ 4個	よんまい 4枚	よんはい 4杯
ごにん 5人	ごこ 5個	ごまい 5枚	ごはい 5杯
ろくにん 6人	ろっこ 6個	ろくまい 6枚	ろっぱい 6杯
ななにん 7人	ななこ 7個	ななまい 7枚	ななはい 7杯
はちにん 8人	はっこ 8個	はちまい 8枚	はちはい 8杯
きゅうにん 9人	きゅうこ 9個	きゅうまい 9枚	きゅうはい 9杯
じゅうにん 10人	じゅっこ 10個	じゅうまい 10枚	じゅっぱい 10杯
		↑ one sheet of paper two sheets of paper	↑ one bowl of rice two bowls of rice

III

仕事を探す
Job hunting

広告を見ました。

Kōkoku o mimashita.

電話で面接の予約をとるときに言います。

ダイアローグ

F　広告を見ました。
Kōkoku o mimashita.

J　いつ面接にこられますか。
Itsu mensetsu ni korare masu ka?

F　いつでもいいです。
Itu demo ii desu.

J　では明日10時にきてください。
Dewa ashita jyū-ji ni kite kudasai.

求職と求人広告

自分に合った仕事を日本で探すには，まず駅の売店で英字新聞を買ってみることです。たとえば毎週月曜日のジャパン・タイムズにはたくさんの求人広告が載っています。適当な職をみつけたら，その日の午前中に電話しましょう。なぜなら多くの外国人が職を求めているからです。

外国人労働者のために，各県（都道府）の労働基準局内に相談コーナーがあります。

そのほか県別の外国人相談窓口や留学生相談コーナーがあります。観光ビザで働くことはできません。みつかれば強制送還させられます。

I saw your advertisement.

These words are said when you want to make an appointment for a job interview.

Dialog

F **I saw your advertisement.**

J **When can you come in for an interview?**

F **I can come any time.**

J **Please come here at 10 o'clock tomorrow.**

Job hunting and a "help wanted" advertisement

If you are looking for a suitable job in Japan, we recommend that you buy an English-language paper. For example, "The Japan Times" has a lot of advertisements on Monday. If you see a good job in the paper, you should call the company in the morning, otherwise you won't get an interview. Many foreigners are looking for jobs these days.

There is a consulting corner for foreign laborers at the Labor Standard Office in each prefecture.

There are counseling desks for foreigners or foreign students in each prefecture. If you have a tourist visa, you won't be able to work. If it is discovered that you are working without having a work visa, you will be deported.

よろしくお願いします。

Yoroshiku onegai shimasu.

配慮をお願いするていねいなあいさつです。

ダイアローグ

J　どうぞお入はいりください。
　　Dōzo ohairi kudasai.

F　しつれいします。
　　Shitsurei shimasu.

J　お名前をどうぞ。
　　Onamae o dōzo.

F　ジム・トンプソンです。よろしくお願いします。
　　Jimu・Tonpuson.　Yoroshiku onegai shimasu.

第一印象が大事

面接を受ける際，態度や服装はとてもたいせつな要素です。ジーンズではなく，男性はスーツにネクタイ，女性はスカートかワンピースにしましょう。コートを着たままイスにかけたり，いきなり足を組むのもやめましょう。

日本人社会では礼儀正しさが好まれます。約束の時間を守り，人と人との出会いをたいせつにしましょう。

人それぞれ性格は異なるし，国民性も異なります。要はまじめで信頼性がある人なら，協力しあっていきたい，また会社としてスポンサーになってもいいと思うでしょう。日本で働きたい外国人は，スポンサーを探すのが第一優先。ワーキングビザが取得できるし，生活が保障されるからです。

Yoroshiku onegai shimasu.

This is a polite way of asking for some kind of consideration.

Dialog

J **Please come in.**

F **Thank you very much.**

J **May I ask your name?**

F **My name is Jim Thompson. Yoroshiku onegai shimasu.**

First impressions are very important.

Your attitude and appearance are important when you have an interview. Men should wear suits, not jeans, and women should wear a skirt or a dress. Don't sit down with a coat on or sit cross-legged straight away.

Politeness is very important in Japanese society. You should be punctual as well.

There are many different types of people, with different personalities and characters, but if you are sincere and reliable you will make a good impression with your desired employer, and he might be willing to become your sponsor. Foreign people who want to stay and work for Japanese companies for a while should find a sponsor as soon as possible. This person will enable you to obtain a work visa so that you will have security and can get on with your life without worry.

いまの日本語わかりません。

Imano nihongo wakari masen.

難しい質問がきたら，こう答えましょう。

ダイアローグ

J　履歴書はお持ちですか。
Rirekisho wa omochi desu ka.

F　すみません。いまの日本語わかりません。
Sumimasen.Imano nihongo wakari masen.

J　この紙に住所・氏名・電話番号を書いてください。
Kono kami ni jūsho・shimei・denwa-bango o kaite kudasai.

F　あのー，やっぱり英語でお願いします。
Anō, yappari eigo de onegai shimasu.

日本で暮らすなら日本語を学ぼう

日本人といっしょに働く以上は，どうしても最低限の日本語がわからなくてはいけません。

コンピューター・プログラマー，エンジニア，デザイナー，銀行・証券マン，医師，弁護士なども日本語は必要です。

パートタイマーでも日本語が少しできると，喫茶店，食堂，弁当屋，スーパーマーケットなど安定した職場が見つかります。

日本語がよくわからない人は，あまり日本語を話す必要のない単純作業から始めることが多いようです。仕事の合間に日本人と積極的に接して，ことばを覚えましょう。

I don't understand that Japanese phrase very well.

If you are asked difficult questions, answer like this.

Dialog

J **Do you have your resume?**

F **I'm sorry. I don't understand that Japanese phrase very well.**

J **Please write down your name, telephone number and address.**

F **Would you mind repeating that in English, please?**

Now that you are living in Japan why not study the Japanese language?

You must understand some basic Japanese because in most jobs in Japan, you will work with Japanese people.

Computer programmers, engineers, designers, bankers (tellers), brokers, doctors, lawyers and so on; they all require some ability in Japanese.

If you can speak a little Japanese you can get long-term part-time jobs at restaurants, cafés, lunchbox parlors, and supermarkets.

Most foreigners who have little Japanese ability will have to start with work which is monotonous at first. Gather a circle of Japanese friends and try to communicate with them in Japanese.

日本語学校に行ってます。

Nihongo-gakkō ni itte masu.

「何をしているか」と聞かれたときに答えることばです。

ダイアローグ

J　いまなにをしてますか。
Ima nani o shite masu ka?

F　日本語学校に行ってます。
Nihongo-gakkō ni itte masu.

J　学校は毎日ですか。
Gakkō wa mainichi desu ka?

F　はい，午前中だけですが。
Hai,gozen-chū dake desu ga.

日本語学校について

最近とくに日本語学校に通う外国人が増えています。日本の短大・大学に留学しようとする人は，かならず事前に日本語学校で勉強しています。日本でしばらく滞在し仕事をしようとする人たちも熱心に通っています。日本語ができれば就職口も広がるからです。

日本の大都市や外国人が多く住んでいる街には日本語を教える学校もしくはボランティア団体があります。正規の日本語学校では学生のためのビザがもらえますが卒業すると資格はなくなります。

I go to a Japanese language school.

This is the answer when you are asked, "What are you doing now?"

Dialog

J	**What do you do at present?**
F	**I go to a Japanese language school.**
J	**Do you go every day?**
F	**Yes, but only in the morning.**

About Japanese language schools

Lately more and more foreigners are attending Japanese language schools. People who intend studying at Japanese junior colleges or universities usually attend a Japanese language school before entering those schools, as do people who want to stay and work in Japan.

Big cities and cities which have many foreign residents have Japanese language institutes or volunteer teaching groups.

Language schools which are approved can provide a student visa, but it will expire when you graduate.

2年は，いるつもりです。

Ninen wa, iru tsumori desu.

日本での滞在期間を答えるときに言います。

ダイアローグ

J　日本にどのくらいいるつもりですか。
Nihon ni dono-kurai iru tsumori desu ka.

F　2年は，いるつもりです。
Ni-nen wa, iru tsumori desu.

J　働きながら何かするつもりですか。
Hataraki nagara nanika suru tsumori desu ka?

F　合気道を勉強します。
Aiki-dō o benkyō shimasu.

異国で働くには我慢が必要

日本の雇用主が外国人を雇いたがらない理由は，じきに辞めて本国へ帰ってしまう人が多かったからです。日本は物価も高く，ことばも不自由で生活しにくい面が数多くあると思います。しかし，本国とは条件のちがう日本で働くには，あるていどの我慢をしなければなりません。

せっかく日本に来たのです。じっくり腰をすえて，自分の国とどこが違うか，なぜ違うのかを学びましょう。未知なるものへの挑戦，それは勇気です。

日本を好きになるか，それとも嫌いになるか，それはあなた次第です。チャレンジあるのみです。

I'm going to stay here for 2 years.

You will answer with these words when talking about the period you intend staying in Japan.

Dialog

J	**How long are you going to stay in Japan?**
F	**I'm going to stay here for 2 years.**
J	**What are you going to do besides working?**
F	**I'm going to learn aikidō.**

You have to be patient when you work in Japan.

The reason Japanese employers don't want to employ foreigners is that they tend to return to their own countries within a short time. Japan is quite an expensive country in which there are a lot of difficult aspects tolife, including the Japanese language. But you have to be patient when working in a foreign country and dealing with a different culture.

Now you are in Japan. Try to settle in and appreciate the different aspects of Japan, comparing them with your country and find out why they differ. It takes courage to face up to unknown things.

どんな仕事ですか。

Donna shigoto desuka?

仕事の内容を確かめるときに言います。

ダイアローグ

F　どんな仕事ですか。
Donna shigoto desu ka?

J　はじめは洗い場です。
Hajime wa araiba desu.

F　何時から何時までですか。
Nanji kara nanji made desu ka?

J　夕方５時から９時までで，時給７００円です。
Yūgata goji kara kuji made de, jikyū nanahyaku-en desu.

コミュニケーションは具体的な表現で

国際学会に世界の言語学者が東京に集まりました。夜のパーティーで各国の学者がひきつづき言語学理論の意見を交わしましたが，内容が抽象的なため，ついに意見は通じませんでした。

同じころ，世界のバーテンダーの集まりがありました。日本の代表は，自分の考えたカクテルの説明を単語だけで言い，そのあと実演をやって大きな拍手を受けました。

会話はどの国のことばでも，具体的な内容のほうが理解しやすいものです。仕事も具体的なことから始めていけば，日本語もすぐ覚えられます。

What exactly does the job entail?

Use these words when you want to check the details of the job.

Dialog

F **What exactly does the job entail?**

J **Washing plates at first.**

F **From what time to what time?**

J **From 5 o'clock until 9 o'clock, and the hourly rate is 700 yen.**

Communication should be held in a tangible way.

The worldwide association of philologists gathered in Tokyo for a meeting. In the evening, there was a party and the scholars from various countries had a drawn-out discussion on linguistic theories, but the contents of the discussion were quite abstract, so their opinions were not understood completely.

At the same time, there was a bartenders' gathering. The bartender representing Japan made and explained his cocktail in halting English and then won some applause.

It is easier to understand people, whatever language is used, when they are talking about concrete things. Likewise, it will be easier for you to learn Japanese if you study concrete facts. Starting from a concrete point, your Japanese ability will improve rapidly.

明日からでもいいです。

Ashita kara demo ii desu.

採用が決まったり，いつから働けるか答えるときに言います。

ダイアローグ

J　いつから働けますか。
Itsu kara hatarake masu ka?

F　明日からでもいいです。
Ashita kara demo ii desu.

J　では来週月曜日，朝９時にきてください。
Dewa raishū getsu-yōbi,asa ku-ji ni kite kudasai.

F　はい，わかりました。
Hai,wakari mashita.

まじめな社員は職場の宝

遅刻しないために目覚まし時計は持っていますか。職場への所要時間はわかっていますか。健康には気をつけていますか。飲みすぎ，遊びすぎ，寝不足はからだをこわすもとです。

毎日職場に行くのが楽しいという人は，精神が安定し，仕事に前向きになっている証拠です。また日本人と接していくのが楽しいと思う人もそうです。ここは日本ですから，日本を積極的に受けいれていこうと自分に言い聞かせてください。仕事を一生けんめいやる人は，まわりの人から好かれます。そして日本人からどんどん話しかけられるでしょう。「帰りに一杯やろう」なんて言われたらもう最高です。

I can start from tomorrow.

You should use these words when you are employed and explaining your available times.

Dialog

J When can you start work?

F I can start from tomorrow.

J Could you come to work on Monday next week at 9 o'clock?

F Yes, certainly.

An earnest employee is a treasure at work.

Do you have an alarm clock so that you won't be late? Do you know how long it takes to get from your home to your office? Are you health conscious? Don't drink too much, and sleep well. Otherwise, your health will suffer.

If you are happy going to work every day, it's a sign of a good mental outlook and a positive attitude to work, and you will enjoy contact with Japanese people as well. Tell yourself that this is Japan, not your hometown, and learn to appreciate the special things about Japan. Your hard work on the job will be appreciated by your colleagues. The Japanese staff will start talking to you. Maybe you will be asked to drink with them after work.

車の修理をしていました。

Kuruma no shūri o shite imashita.

何の仕事をしていたか聞かれたときに答えることばです。

ダイアローグ

J　お国ではあなたは何をしていましたか。
Okuni dewa anatawa nani o shite imashita ka?

F　車の修理をしていました。
Kuruma no shūri o shite imashita.

J　そのほか，なにか。
Sono hoka,nanika?

F　経理も少しできます。
Keiri mo sukoshi dekimasu.

日本人が就職するのもたいへん

日本の会社の採用条件は，学歴・年齢が優先されることがあります。最終学歴は一流大学ほど有利です。専攻は文化系か技術系かで大別されます。女性だからといって差別はしませんが，結婚・出産という場合，退職・休暇という事態になり，会社としては戦力を失うことになりますから，それを心配する会社もあります。

つぎに必要な条件は，やる気・協調性・明るさ・まじめ，といった人間性です。健康であることも大切な要素です。

I was a car repairman.

Use this kind of statement when questioned about your former occupation.

Dialog

J **What were you doing before in your hometown?**

F **I was a car repairman.**

J **Anything else?**

F **I did a little work in accounts.**

It is hard to find employment, even for the Japanese.

In choosing employees, the Japanese company will take into consideration such factors as the university you attended and your age. The rank of the last university attended is considered to be of most importance. There are roughly two are as in which students can major :the sciences and the liberal arts. Women are not discriminated against, but some companies may hesitate to employ them as, in the event of marriage and childbirth, they may leave the company. The next important factors will be human qualities such as positiveness, co-operativeness, an open character and sincerity. Being in a state of good health is another important consideration.

あのー，給料日はいつですか。

Anō, kyūryō-bi wa itsu desu ka?

給料日を確かめるときに言います。

ダイアローグ

F　あのー，給料日はいつですか。
Anō,kyūryō-bi wa itsu desu ka?

J　毎月２５日です。
Maitsuki nijyū-go-nichi desu.

F　現金ですか。
Genkin desu ka?

J　銀行振り込みです。
Ginkō furikomi desu.

ワリカンでやきとり屋へ

日本のビジネスマンは，よく会社の帰りに仲間を誘ってお酒を飲みに行きます。仕事によるストレスの解消のためです。

もし，飲みに誘われたら，日本人の仲間入りをするチャンスです。日本語も上達するし，仕事の上での人間関係もうまくいくでしょう。

誘った人が支払うこともありますが，自分の分は出す用意をしておきましょう。仲間同士のワリカンのほうが長いつきあいができます。

Well, which day is payday?

You can check your payday using these words.

Dialog

F	**Well, which day is payday?**
J	**On the 25th of every month.**
F	**Do you pay in cash?**
J	**We pay into your bank account.**

Going Dutch at a *yakitori* bar

Japanese businessmen often go out to drink after work together with their friends or colleagues. This acts as a catharsis for work stress.

If you are invited to this kind of occasion, it is a good opportunity to get to know the Japanese. You can improve your Japanese and your relationships on the job.

The person who invites you might pay the bill but you should always be prepared to pay. If you want good long-term relationships you should pay separately.

職業（しょくぎょう）の種類（しゅるい）　Berufe

外交官（がいこうかん）　diplomat

弁護士（べんごし）　lawyer

医師（いし）　medical doctor

歯科医（しかい）　dentist

公認会計士（こうにんかいけいし）　accountant

（米）certified public accountant(C.P.A.)

（英）chartered accountant

ファンドマネジャー　fund manager

コンサルタント　consultant

銀行員（ぎんこういん）　bank clerk

技師（ぎし）　engineer

システム・エンジニア　systems engineer

プログラマー　computer programmer

ジャーナリスト　Journalist

編集者（へんしゅうしゃ）　editor

アーティスト　artist

音楽家（おんがくか）　musician

芸能人（げいのうじん）　entertainer

ビジネスマン　businessman

会社役員（かいしゃやくいん）　director, executive

会社員（かいしゃいん）　company employee, office worker

公務員（こうむいん）　government clerk

大学教授（だいがくきょうじゅ）　professor

教師（きょうし）　teacher

外国語教師（がいこくごきょうし）　Language teacher

建築家（けんちくか）　architect

農業（のうぎょう）　farming

漁業（ぎょぎょう）　fishing

商店経営者（しょうてんけいえいしゃ）　shop owner

卸売業者（おろしうりぎょうしゃ）　whole saler

小売業者（こうりぎょうしゃ）　retailer

金融業（きんゆうぎょう）　financial business

メーカー　manufacturer

商社（しょうしゃ）　trading company

貿易（ぼうえき）　foreign trade

流通（りゅうつう）　distribution

運輸（うんゆ）　transportation

パートタイマー　part-timer

学生（がくせい）　student

IV

毎日の生活
Everyday life

おはようございます。

Ohayō gozaimasu.

朝のあいさつです。

ダイアローグ

F　おはようございます。
　　Ohayō gozaimasu.

J　おはよう，ナンシー。もう会社。
　　Ohayō, Nanshi. Mō kaisha?

F　はい。では，いってきます。
　　Hai. Dewa, itte kimasu.

J　気をつけて，いってらっしゃい。
　　Ki o tsukete, itte rasshai.

目上の人にはていねいに

お年寄が「おはよう」と声をかけてきても，同じように「おはよう」と答えてはいけません。目上の人にはていねいに「おはようございます」と言います。どの国のことばにもていねいな言いかたはありますが，日本の敬語の使いかたはとくに複雑です。日本人でも上手に使い分けできる人が少ないといわれています。しかし，外国人だからどうでもいいということではありません。ていねいな言葉遣いをすれば，かならず人に好かれます。

日本語には女性特有の言いまわしがあるし，若者独特の表現もあり，狭い日本にも数多くの方言があります。

Good morning.

This is a greeting used in the morning.

Dialog

F **Good morning.**

J **Good morning, Nancy. Off to work already?**

F **Yes, bye.**

J **Take care, bye.**

Be polite to elderly people.

If your elderly neighbor greets you with "*Ohayō.*", do not answer in like manner, "*Ohayō*". You should answer "*Ohayō gozaimasu*" politely. Every language has polite expressions, but especially in Japanese, polite expressions have very particular uses. Even the Japanese don't always use them perfectly. But you shouldn't give up trying to master their use because it can impress people very favorably if you can use polite expressions correctly. The Japanese language has special women's expressions and young people's expressions. There are also local dialects in this small country of Japan.

ただいま。

Tadaima.

帰ったときのあいさつです。

ダイアローグ

J　あら，ナンシー，おかえりなさい。
Ara, Nanshi, okaeri nasai.

F　ただいま。
Tadaima.

J　お仕事おつかれさま。
Oshigoto otsukaresama.

F　どうも。
Dō mo.

留守宅配達の宅配便・書留郵便

留守中に宅配便や書留郵便が配達された場合は，「不在配達通知書」がポストに入れられます。

留守宅の場合，「①〜さんのお宅に預けました」「②都合のいい日時を電話でお知らせください」などと書いてあります。

書留郵便の場合，「①都合のいい日を書いてポストに入れてください」「②明日以降，身分証明・印鑑持参の上，本局に取りにきてください」とあります。日曜日は配達しません。急ぎの場合，本局までパスポートを持って受け取りに行きます。平日は夜8時まで，土・日なら5時までです。わからなかったらお隣の人に聞きましょう。

I'm back.

This is a greeting when you come home from somewhere.

Dialog

J Ah, you are back, Nancy.

F Yes, I'm back.

J Had a hard day?

F Well, not so bad.

Special delivery and registered mail came while you were out.

A letter informing you of a delivery while you were out is called a "Fuzai haitatsu" letter. It is usually put in your letter box if parcels or registered mail are delivered while you are out.

Notice of delivery service is usually written like, '①Delivery is left at Mr. or Mrs. ～.' or '②Please let us know a convenient time to deliver.' Registered mail is '①Post this notice after you write a convenient time to deliver.' '②Please come to the main post office with your identity card and seal.' There is no delivery on Sunday. If you are in a hurry, you should go to the main post with your passport. Weekdays: open until 8 o'clock; weekend: open until 5 o'clock. If you can't understand something, ask your neighbors.

こんばんは。

Konban wa.

暗（くら）くなってからかわすあいさつです。

ダイアローグ

F　こんばんは，鈴木（すずき）さん。
Konban wa, Suzuki-san.

J　いまお帰（かえ）り。ちょっとお茶（ちゃ）でもどう。
Ima okaeri? Chotto ochademo dō?

F　いいえ，もう休（やす）みますから。
Iie, mō yasumi masukara.

J　あら，そう。じゃ，おやすみなさい。
Ara, sō. Jā, oyasumi nasai.

日用必需品（にちようひつじゅひん）の買（か）いかた

日本で暮（く）らしていくためには，日用必需品をいろいろそろえなければなりません。

冷蔵庫（れいぞうこ）・暖房器具（だんぼうきぐ）・家具類（かぐるい）は中古品（ちゅうこひん）や不要品（ふようひん）の買（か）えるバザーがあります。急（いそ）ぎならディスカウント・ストアで探（さが）します。運（うん）がよければ国へ帰る外国人から直接（ちょくせつ）いろいろな品を超特価（ちょうとっか）で買（か）える場合（ばあい）もあります。食器（しょっき）・鍋類（なべるい）・衣料品（いりょうひん）・食料品（しょくりょうひん）などはスーパー（マーケット）が便利（べんり）です。スーパーでは買（か）い物（もの）カゴに品物（しなもの）を入れ，最後（さいご）にレジで支払（しはら）いをします。包装（ほうそう）は日本語だけの表示（ひょうじ）が多いので，砂糖（さとう）か塩（しお）か，洗剤（せんざい）かシャンプーかよく確（たし）かめて買（か）ってください。

Good evening.

A greeting for after dark.

Dialog

F **Good evening, Ms. Suzuki.**

J **You're home. Would you like a cup of tea?**

F **No, thank you. I'm going to bed now.**

J **Alright then. Good night.**

How to buy daily necessities.

You will need many things for your everyday life. There is a marketplace where you can buy second-hand refrigerators, heaters, and furniture. If you need things immediately, you can go to a discount shop. If you are lucky, you may have a chance to go to a garage sale, many of which are held by people going back to their own countries. Tableware, cooking utensils, clothes, and food are sold at supermarkets at reasonable prices.

At the supermarket, you use a basket to carry your items and you pay at the cash register. You should check that you have the right things as the labels are written in Japanese.

これでいいですか。

Korede ii desu ka?

確認(かくにん)するときの言(い)いかたです。

ダイアローグ

F　いっしょに持(も)っていきましょうか。
　　Isshoni motte ikimashō ka.

J　どうも。今日(きょう)は缶(かん)の日(ひ)ですよね。
　　Dōmo. Kyō wa kan-no hi desu yone.

F　ええ。これで，いいですか。
　　Ee. Korede ii desu ka?

J　ええ。だいじょうぶです。
　　Ee. Daijōbu desu.

公衆電話(こうしゅうでんわ)のかけかた

日本の電話料金(でんわりょうきん)は，時間(じかん)・距離(きょり)によって異(こと)なります。同区域内(どうくいきない)（市(し)・町内(ちょうない)）でも長(なが)く話(はな)すと料金が加算(かさん)されていきます。区域外(くいきがい)（市外(しがい)）にかけるときは地区コード番号(ばんごう)からダイヤルします。

公衆電話を使うときは，まず受話器(じゅわき)を取(と)り，市内(しない)なら１０円，市外(しがい)で近距離(きんきょり)は１０円玉を３つ～５つ，長距離(ちょうきょり)なら１００円を入れて，ツーという音(おと)を聞(き)いてからダイヤルします。よく電話をかける人は，テレフォンカードを買っておくと便利(べんり)です。１枚(まい)５００円（１０円×５０回）と1,０００円（１０円×１０５回）があり，使用するときに残(のこ)りの度数(どすう)が電話機(でんわき)に表示(ひょうじ)されます。使用方法(しようほうほう)は受話器を取ってからカードをカード挿入口(そうにゅうぐち)に入れ，ダイヤルし，通話(つうわ)が終わって受話器を置くと，ピーという音がしてカードが下から出てきます。

Is this alright?

This is a expression to confirm things.

Dialog

F **Shall I take your rubbish with mine to the collection place?**

J **Yes, thank you. Today is can day, isn't it?**

F **Yes, it is. Is this alright? Have I organized my rubbish properly?**

J **Yes, you've done it the right way.**

How to use a public telephone.

Japanese telecommunication charges depend on time and distance. Within your own area, if you talk for longer than the set period, you will be charged more. When you call an outside area, start with the area code. When you use a public telephone, take the receiver and insert a coin. (Within the city 10 yen, outside the city three or four 10 yen coins, long distance 100 yen coins). After hearing a "tsū-" sound start dialing. If you use public telephones frequently, you should buy a telephone card. There are 500 yen cards (10 yen × 50 times) and 1,000 yen cards (10 yen × 105 times). It will be indicated on the phone how many points you have left when you insert the card. In the same manner as when you use coins, pick up the receiver first, then, insert the card and dial. When you have finished your call, replace the receiver. The card will come out with a "pi-" sound.

いま，何時ですか。

Ima, nanji desuka?

時間(じかん)をたずねるときの言(い)いかたです。

ダイアローグ

F　いま，何時(なんじ)ですか。
Ima, nanji desu ka?

J　午後(ごご)の３時(さんじ)です。
Gogo no san-ji desu.

F　わたしの国(くに)は，たぶん夜(よる)の１０時(じゅうじ)です。
Watashino kuni wa, tabun yoru no jyū-ji desu.

J　国際電話(こくさいでんわ)をかけるんでしょう。
Kokusai denwa o kakerun deshō?

国際電話(こくさいでんわ)のかけかた

直接海外(ちょくせつかいがい)にかけるときは，001を回(まわ)し，つづいて国番号(くにばんごう)・市外局番(しがいきょくばん)・電話番号(でんわばんごう)をダイヤルします。

例(れい)：001（国際(こくさい)コード）－1（国番号）－212（市外局番）－123－4567

交換手(こうかんしゅ)を呼(よ)び出してかける方法(ほうほう)もあります。

料金(りょうきん)は時間帯(じかんたい)によっては割(わ)り引(び)きがあります。

ITJ，IDC という特定国(とくていこく)への国際電話会社(こくさいでんわがいしゃ)や，カードで国際電話がかけられる公衆電話(こうしゅうでんわ)もあります。

What time is it now?

Used when you want to know the time.

Dialog

F **What time is it now?**

J **3 o'clock in the afternoon.**

F **In my country it's probably 10 o'clock.**

J **You call outside Japan, don't you?**

How to make an international telephone call.

When you wish to call outside Japan dial 001, the country code, the area code, and the telephone number.

Example: 001 (IDD)-1 (country code)-212 (area code)-123-4567

There is another way to make an international call in which you call through an operator. The telephone charge is discounted depending on the hour.

There are other international telephone companies like ITJ and IDC which service specific countries. Also, there are public telephones from which you can make an international telephone call with a telephone card.

これはなんですか。

Kore wa nandesu ka?

物の名前などを聞くときに使います。

ダイアローグ

F　これはなんですか。
Kore wa nandesu ka?

J　鳥居です。これが神社です。
Tori-i desu. Kore ga jinja desu.

F　あれはなんですか。
Are wa nandesu ka?

J　あれはお寺の山門です。
Are wa otera no sanmon desu.

教会と礼拝について

日本には各地にお寺や神社があります。お寺には必ず屋根のある門があり，本堂に仏像が安置されています。神社は日本の神をまつっています。神社には必ず鳥居があります。

日本に住む外国人が，自分の信仰のため毎週教会に行きたくても，キリスト教以外の礼拝堂を探すのは難しいでしょう。自室に簡単な礼拝所を作ったり，決まった日に断食をしている人もいるようです。

What is this?

Used when you ask the names of goods.

Dialog

F What is this?

J It's a '*torii*'. (shrine gate)

F What is that?

J It's the main gate of a temple.

Churches and services

There are shrines and temples, here and there, all over Japan. Every temple has a gate, with a roof on it, and there is a statue of Buddha enshrined in the main building. Japanese people worship the gods at a shrine which has a specially shaped gate called a '*torii*' in front of it.

The foreigners in Japan come from all over the world and have many different religions. But it is very difficult for most of them (except the Christians) to attend their own religious services in Japan.

Some people make their own simple altars, or fast, according to the demands of their particular religion.

おいそがしいですか。

Oisogashii desu ka?

本当にいそがしいかどうかを聞くのではなく，これもひとつのあいさつです。

ダイアローグ

J　あら，カーリン。お久しぶりね。
Ara, Karin. Ohisasiburi ne.

F　おいそがしいですか。
Oisogasii desu ka?

J　いいえ。ところで，どちらへ。
Iie. Tokoro de, dochira e?

F　ちょっと，美容院へ。
Chotto, biyō-in e.

美容院と理髪店

美容院も理髪店も，近所で行きつけの店をつくっておくと便利です。こちらの好みがわかるからです。お店によっては担当者を指名することもできるし，電話で予約もとれます。日本ではチップは必要ありません。

日本語に「馬子にも衣装，髪かたち」ということわざがあります。髪をととのえ，きれいなかっこうをすればどんな人でもりっぱに見えるという意味です。

仕事をする日本人はそれなりに服装・髪かたちを気にしています。衣服はいつもクリーニングし，毎日アイロンをかけます。女性は美容院へ，男性は理髪店へ平均月１回は行きます。

Are you busy?

This is a simple everyday greeting and is not intended to be a serious question as to whether the person is really busy or not.

Dialog

J **Oh, hello, Karen. Long time no see.**

F **Are you busy?**

J **No. By the way where are you going?**

F **I'm going to the hairdresser.**

Hairdresser and barber shop

If you have a regular hairdresser or barber, it is convenient, because they can get to know what suits you. You can call your favorite hairdresser and make an appointment by telephone. You don't need to tip in Japan.

There is a proverb 'Even a pack horse driver looks respectable in fine clothes', which means the same as 'Fine feathers make a fine bird'. A person can look good if he dresses well. Professional Japanese take pride in their appearance and strive to be well-groomed. Their clothes are always clean and ironed. The Japanese go to a hairdresser or barber shop once a month on average.

どういたしまして。

Dō itashi mashite.

お礼を言われたときの返事のしかたです。

ダイアローグ

J　この間はどうも。
Kono aida wa dōmo.

F　えっ。
Eh?

J　先日はお菓子をありがとうございました。
Senjitsu wa okashi o arigatōgozai mashita.

F　いいえ，どういたしまして。
Iie, dō itashi mashite.

お礼をくり返す日本人

日本人は，親切にしてもらったり，プレゼントをもらうと，すぐにお礼を言いますが，後日会ったときにも「この間はどうも」とまたお礼を言います。

外国人にとって，「この間は」とか「先日は」がいつのことかさっぱりわからないことがあるようです。しかし，くり返しお礼を言うのが日本人の礼儀にもなっています。

外国人は別れるとき，精いっぱいお礼を言ってそれで終わりです。日本人はほめ言葉や感謝の表現があまり上手ではないので，別れるとき何度もおじぎをしているようです。

You're welcome. (Not at all.)

How to acknowledge expressions of gratitude.

Dialog

J **Thank you very much for the other day.**

F **I beg your pardon?**

J **Thank you for the confectionery the other day.**

F **Oh, not at all. You are welcome.**

The Japanese repeatedly express their gratitude.

Japanese people express their gratitude when they are given presents or treated favorably. Besides that, they say "Thanks for the other day." when they meet each other again.

Foreigners sometimes have no idea what the Japanese are talking about when they say "last time" or "the other day". But repeating their gratitude is a Japanese courtesy.

Usually foreigners express thanks once, as best as they can. Since Japanese people are not good at praising or expressing their gratitude, they tend to bow many times instead.

銀行自動入出金機 Automatic Teller Machine

預け入れ	deposit
振り替え	transfer
通帳記入	passbook update
引き出し	withdrawal
振り込み	remittance (payment)
残高照会	account balance
万	10,000 yen notes
千	1,000 yen notes
円	yen
確認	Press this key for confirmation.
訂正	Press this key if you want to make a correction.
手続き取消	Press this key if you want to cancel the transaction.

V

交通機関の利用
Using public transport

JRの地図はありますか。

Jei-āru no chizu wa arimasu ka?

路線図をもらうときの言いかたです。

ダイアローグ

F　JRの地図はありますか。
Jei-āru no chizu wa arimasu ka?

J　どこへ行きますか。
Doko e ikimasu ka?

F　六本木です。
Roppongi desu.

J　それなら地下鉄ですね。
Sorenara chikatetsu desu ne.

まず路線図を手に入れよう

交通機関を利用するときは，まず路線図を手に入れましょう。JRや地下鉄は，どの駅でも無料でもらえます。くわしい地図が欲しいなら，書店でバイリンガル（英日）か英文のものを買ってください。地図が頭に入っていると行動しやすくなります。場所によっては，その町の英文地図があります。

大都市周辺は私鉄が発達しています。急ぐときには，交通渋滞が予想されるので，鉄道を利用するほうが確実です。日本の鉄道は時刻表どおり運行されているので安心です。

Could I have a JR map?

When you ask for a map, use this expression.

Dialog

F **Could I have a JR map?**

J **Where do you want to go?**

F **I'm going to Roppongi.**

J **You can go by subway. So you'll need a subway map.**

First of all get a transport map.

Before you use the public transport system, get a map. You can get one free at any JR or subway station. If you need a detailed map, you can buy a bilingual (English/Japanese) atlas or English map at a bookstore. It will be easier to find your way around if you study the map a little, before setting out. Some towns prepare maps written in English.

Many private lines have developed around big cities. When you are in a hurry, you should use the railway, as it is more reliable than a car because of traffic jams. Japanese railways are very punctual and reliable.

渋谷までいくらですか。

Shibuya made ikura desu ka?

切符の値段がわからないときの聞きかたです。

ダイアローグ

F　渋谷までいくらですか。
Shibuya made ikura desu ka?

J　180円です。
Hyaku-hachijū-en desu.

F　乗り換えはありますか。
Norikae wa arimasu ka?

J　新宿で12番線に乗り換えてください。
Shinjuku de jū-ni-ban-sen ni norikaete kudasai.

乗車券の買いかた

駅の乗車券売り場には料金表がありますが，どれも日本語だけなので，わからないときはすぐそばの日本人に「～までいくらですか」と聞いてください。

乗車券を買うには，自動切符販売機にお金を入れるか，プリペイド・カードで買う方法があります。JR用はSuicaといいます。地下鉄用はいろいろ呼び方があります。

いつも決まった区間を利用する人は，回数券，長期利用者は定期券（1か月分・3か月分・6か月分）を買うと得になります。

How much is it to Shibuya?

For when you want to know the cost of a ticket.

Dialog

F **How much is it to Shibuya?**

J **It's 180 yen.**

F **Do I have to change anywhere?**

J **Please change at Shinjuku. Take a train from platform No. 12.**

How to buy a ticket.

There are usually large lists of fares for the rail system at the railway station. But often they are written in Japanese, so ask a nearby Japanese "How much is it to ——"

You can buy a ticket by inserting money or prepaid cards into the ticket machine. The Suica Card is used for JR only. Subway cards have various names. If you use the same rail route frequently, buying a coupon ticket will save you a little money. Commuters and students should use the (1 month, 3 month or 6 month) commuter's pass (rail pass) which is again, considerably cheaper.

池袋に行きますか。

Ikebukuro ni ikimasu ka?

バスに乗るときに行き先を確かめる言いかたです。

ダイアローグ

F　これは池袋に行きますか。
　　Kore wa Ikebukuro ni ikimasu ka?

J　はい，ここから3つ目，終点です。
　　Hai, koko kara mittsu-me, shūten desu.

F　いくらですか。
　　Ikura desu ka?

J　180円。ここに入れてください。
　　Hyaku-hachi-jū-en. Koko ni irete kudasai.

バスの利用のしかた

大都市にかぎらず地方都市でも，駅前のバスターミナルにはたくさんのバスが止まっています。どこを通ってどこまで行くのか，ほとんど漢字で書いてあります。日本人に確かめるしかありません。バス料金は全線均一のところもあるし，距離によって料金が加算されていくところもあります。前者の場合は前払い，後者の場合は後払いですが，途中から乗車するときは区間番号切符を取ってから乗らないと始発からの料金を取られます。

コインの持ち合わせがないときは，料金入れのわきに両替機がついています。

Do you go to Ikebukuro?
(Does this bus go to Ikebukuro?)

Make sure that the bus you take goes to your desired destination.

Dialog

F Do you go to Ikebukuro? (Does this bus go to Ikebukuro?)

J Yes, it's the third stop from here and it's the last stop.

F How much is it?

J It's 180 yen. Deposit the coins in here.

How to use a bus.

In big cities, as well as small cities, there are many buses stopping at the bus terminals. The directions are all written in Japanese. You will need to check with Japanese. Some buses charge a flat rate, but some charge according to the distance traveled. In the former system, payment is made when you get on the bus, and in the latter system, payment is made when you get off the bus, according to the ticket you take on entering the bus. If you forget to take this ticket, you will have to pay the full fare. If you don't have any small change, you can change a note to small change at the exchange machine attached to the payment machine.

どうしたらいいですか。

Dō shitara ii desu ka?

方法をたずねる言いかたです。

ダイアローグ

F　北海道へ行きたいのですが。
Hokkaidō e ikitaino desu ga.

J　それはいいですね。
Sore wa ii desune.

F　どうしたらいいですか。
Dō shitara ii desu ka?

J　旅行代理店に相談したら。
Ryokō-dairiten ni sōdan shitara?

旅行代理店を利用しよう

新幹線や飛行機を利用するときは近くの旅行代理店で予約ができます。英語も通じるところが多くあります。切符を購入するだけでなく，旅行の相談にも応じてくれます。スケジュールに合わせてコースを推せんしてくれたり，予算にあったホテル・日本旅館の予約もしてくれます。これらはいっさい手数料もチップもいりません。

シーズンに適した旅行企画のカタログやいろいろな資料もそろっています。説明を聞いたあとでゆっくり検討するのもいいでしょう。週末はどこも混雑しますから，早目に計画を立てましょう。

How should I go about it?

The way to ask the method of doing something.

Dialog

F **I'd like to go to Hokkaidō.**

J **That's a nice idea.**

F **How should I go about it?**

J **What about consulting a travel agency?**

Make use of travel agency.

When you use the *Shinkansen* or a plane, you can book your ticket through a nearby travel agency. The people who work at a travel agency often understand English. You can consult with them about travel plans, as well as trying your ticket there. They can recommend an efficient itinerary according to your schedule or they can book a hotel or Japanese inn within your budget. There's no need to pay a commission or tip.

They provide brochures (pamphlets) of travel plans for each season, as well as other dates. You can think it over at your leisure after listening to their explanation. You should plan early for weekends.

日本(にほん)の地図(ちず)　Map of Japan

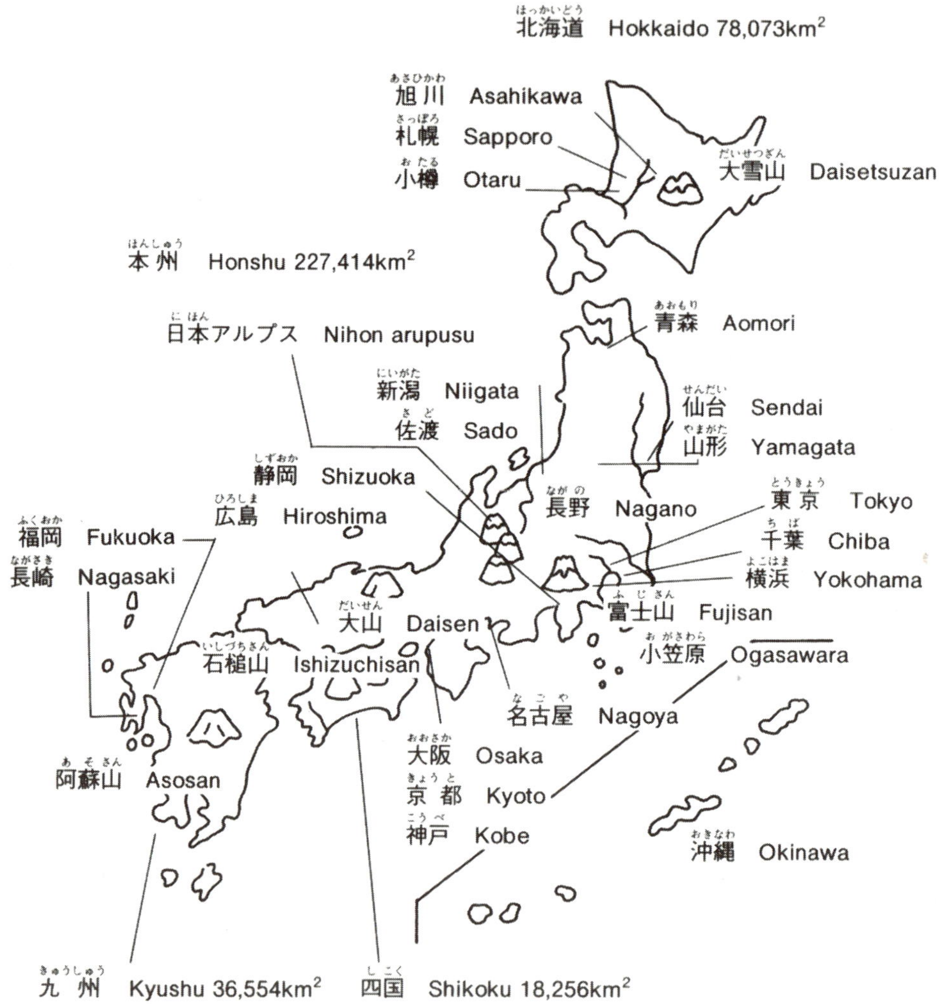

VI

買い物・外食
Shopping and eating out

ツナの缶詰はありますか。

Tsuna no kanzume wa arimasu ka?

小売店で目的の品物があるかどうかたずねるときに言います。

ダイアローグ

J　いらっしゃいませ。
Irasshaimase.

F　ツナの缶詰はありますか。
Tsuna no kanzume wa arimasu ka?

J　ありますよ。大きさは２種類です。
Arimasu yo. Ōkisa wa nishurui desu.

F　小さいほうをください。
Chiisai hō o kudasai.

専門店の買い物を楽しもう

日本にはいろいろな専門店があります。デパートやスーパーが近くにあればいいですが，専門店には近所の便利さと親しみやすさがあるので，ぜひ買い物をするようおすすめします。地域の人たちは英語が話せない人のほうが多いので，日本語の勉強にも役立ちます。

一般食料品店，八百屋，魚屋，豆腐屋，酒屋，すし屋，本屋，花屋，理髪店，美容院，写真屋，薬屋，クリーニング店，靴屋，天ぷら屋，衣料品店，自転車屋，電気店，家具店，レコード店，ペットショップ，喫茶店，テイクアウトショップ，飲み屋，パチンコ屋，ゲームセンター，銭湯，材木店，葬儀屋など，まだたくさんありますから，あなた自身で探してみましょう。

Do you have any canned tuna?

To use when you ask for what you want at a shop.

Dialog

J **Hello. May I help you?**

F **Do you have any canned tuna?**

J **Yes. We have two sizes.**

F **Could I have the smaller one?**

Enjoy shopping at a specialty shop.

Japanese streets have many kinds of specialty shops. Department stores or supermarkets are alright, if you have one near you, but specialty shops are convenient and friendly. It is also good for you to practice your Japanese, as local people don't always speak English.

The grocer, greengrocer, fish market, *tōfu* shop, liquor shop, sushi shop, bookshop, florist, barber, hairdresser, photography studio, drugstore, dry-cleaners, shoe shop, tenpura restaurant, clothing shop, bicycle shop, electric shop, record shop, pet shop, café, take-out shop, bar, pachinko parlor, game center, public bath, timber merchant, funeral parlor: these are all common specialty shops, and there are many more. Find out about these other shops and discover Japan.

やっぱり，これにします。

Yappari, koreni shimasu.

いろいろすすめられ，やっと買う物を決めたときに言います。

ダイアローグ

J　どちらになさいますか。
Dochira ni nasai masuka?

F　ええと，ちょっと待ってください。
Eeto, chotto matte kudasai.

J　これは新しいデザインです。
Kore wa atarashii dezain desu.

F　やっぱり，これにします。
Yappari, koreni shimasu.

日本のデパートのサービスは超一流

日本のデパートは，お客さまへのサービスが，とてもよく行き届いています。

顧客第一という基本精神が「お客様は神様です」の流行語をつくりました。外国の人たちには必要以上のサービス精神とも思われるでしょうが，10時開店と同時にデパートに入ると，店員たちが並んでおじぎをしてお客さまを迎えます。それが良いか悪いかは別として，日本のデパートのサービスから，日本の一面を学んでください。

I'll take this.

When there are many things to choose from and you want a few moments to consider, then you express it this way.

Dialog

J **Which one would you like?**

F **Well, can you wait for a moment, please?**

J **This is a new design.**

F **I'll take this.**

Service in a Japanese department store is first-rate.

The service offered by Japanese department stores to all their customers is of a high level.

The fundamental idea that the customer comes first has developed into the popular phrase 'The customer is God'. Foreigners might feel that Japanese service is more than is needed. If you step into a department store at the 10 o'clock opening time, you will be welcomed with bows from the salesclerks standing in line at the entrance. You may have your own idea on whether or not this custom is desirable, but it exemplifies the spirit of service that exists in Japanese department stores. It is another aspect of Japanese culture.

カメラを買いたいのですが。

Kamera o kaitai no desu ga.

何か を買いに店内に入ったとき店員に言います。

ダイアローグ

F　カメラを買いたいのですが。
Kamera o kaitai no desu ga.

J　どんなカメラでしょうか。
Donna Kamera deshō ka?

F　小さいのがいいです。
Chiisai no ga ii desu.

J　これはいかがでしょうか。
Kore wa ikaga deshō ka?

ディスカウント・ショップを探そう

いま日本ではディスカウント・ショップに人気が集まっています。

東京では秋葉原の電気街が有名ですが，そのほか渋谷・新宿・池袋の駅の近辺には，電気・カメラ・時計その他のディスカウント・ショップが軒並みあります。地方都市にもそれらのチェーン店が進出しています。日本人はもとより外国人もいっぱい来ています。

新宿などの大手チェーン店は，何か国語かで店内放送をしています。休日を利用していちど訪れてみてはいかがでしょう。現金仕入れによる大量販売という流通システムが，低価格の秘密なのです。

I'd like to buy a camera.

When you wish to buy something at a shop, tell the salesclerk what you want.

Dialog

F **I'd like to buy a camera.**

J **What kind of camera would you like?**

F **I want to buy a small one.**

J **How about this?**

Find out about discount shops.

Discount shops are quite popular in Japan now. In Tokyo, Akihabara Electric Street is famous. There are other discount electrical goods shops, camera shops, and so on at nearby stations, such as Shibuya, Shinjuku and Ikebukuro. In many other cities, there are many branches of those Tokyo discount shops. Foreigners can also patronize discount shops.

A big discount shop in Shinjuku announces its information in several languages. Why don't you visit it one holiday?

The reason for the cheap prices in the electrical discount shops is that the shop owner follows a market system, in which he buys in bulk for cash, from a warehouse.

メニューありますか。

Menyū arimasu ka?

レストランでメニューを見(み)たいときに言(い)います。

ダイアローグ

F　メニューありますか。
Menyū arimasu ka?

J　はい，ここにあります。
Hai, koko ni arimasu.

F　これは読(よ)めません。
Kore wa yomemasen.

J　あ，すみません。これは，天(てん)ぷら……。
A, sumimasen. Kore wa tenpura……

外国人(がいこくじん)のための情報誌(じょうほうし)

空港内(くうこうない)には，当面(とうめん)生活するための情報が十分(じゅうぶん)にあり，不動産関係(ふどうさんかんけい)のパンフレットも置(お)いてあります。

ホテルのロビーなどにも無料(むりょう)でもらえる情報誌(じょうほうし)がいくつかあります。観光(かんこう)・行事(ぎょうじ)・映画(えいが)・芸術(げいじゅつ)・レストランガイドなど多彩(たさい)です。また大手書店(おおてしょてん)などには外国人のための生活情報誌(じょうほうし)が並んでいます。あなたの住(す)んでいる街(まち)にも市役所(しやくしょ)などに，外国人向(む)けの情報があるでしょう。

Could I see the menu, please?

Ask for the menu like this.

Dialog

F Could I see the menu, please?

J Yes, here you are.

F I don't undersand this.

J Oh, sorry, this is tenpura....

Information magazines for foreigners

In the airport you can obtain sufficient information which is made for you to use in your life in Japan; besides that, real estate pamphlets are available.

There are free information pamphlets in hotel lobbies. They are of various kinds, such as sight-seeing guides, information about meetings, events, films, art, restaurants, etc. You can also find many magazines containing information for foreigners at large bookstores. You can get information of interest to foreigners at your town's ward office.

これはとてもおいしいですね。

Kore wa totemo oishii desu ne.

味についての感想を言うときに使います。

ダイアローグ

F　これはとてもおいしいですね。
　　Kore wa totemo oishii desu ne.

J　それはありがとうございます。
　　Sore wa arigatō gozaimasu.

F　何という料理ですか。
　　Nanto iu ryōri desu ka.

J　ハヤシライスです。
　　Hayashi-raisu desu.

国際色豊かな日本の食事

日本ではすし，天ぷらなどの日本料理はもちろん，世界の代表的な料理は何でも食べられます。日本人のこどもに人気のあるカレーライスはもともとインドやイギリスから来たものですが，すっかり日本に定着しています。ラーメンやぎょうざも中国からのものですが，日本人の食生活には欠かせません。フランス料理・イタリア料理・スペイン料理・ロシア料理・韓国焼肉店など専門店はどこにもあります。探せばインド料理，カンボジア料理店その他たくさんあります。

また，デパートの食品街や紀ノ国屋などの食料品専門店に行けば，いろいろな国の食品や食材が求められます。テイクアウトの店といえば，マクドナルド，ケンタッキーやお弁当屋さんなど，どこでも看板を見かけます。

This is quite delicious.

Use this when you want to express your enjoyment of food.

Dialog

F **This is quite delicious!**

J **Thank you very much.**

F **What is it called?**

J **It's called *Hayashi raisu*.**

Meals in Japan can be very international!

You can have many of the world's famous dishes in Japan, as well as Japanese dishes, such as *sushi* and *tenpura*. Curry with rice is popular among Japanese children, although it was originally from India and England. There is a Japanese version now. *Rāmen* and *gyōza* were originally from China, but Japanese eat them regularly and they have become indispensable things in our daily menu. You can find special restaurants such as French, Italian, Spanish, Russian, Korean barbecue, etc, everywhere. If you try, you can find Indian, Cambodian and others as well.

If you go to a food floor in a department store or special grocery shop like *Kinokuniya*, you can buy food from many countries. As well, there are take-away shops. You can see their many signs along the street —— McDonald's, Kentucky Fried Chicken, etc.

もっとください。

Motto kudasai.

さらに何か欲しいときに言います。

ダイアローグ

F　これ，もっとください。
　Kore, motto kudasai.

J　やきとり，好きですか。
　Yakitori, suki desu ka?

F　はい。お酒ももう一杯。
　Hai. Osake mo mō ippai.

J　はい，お待ちどうさま。
　Hai, omachidō sama.

何でもトライしてみませんか

日本人がよく食べる物に納豆があります。日本人の中にも嫌いな人がいますし，食べられない外国人もたくさんいます。これは大豆を発酵させて作ったもので，健康食としては最良のものです。ある外国人は納豆を見て「大豆？　100年前の？」と顔をしかめました。またある外国人は一口食べてとても好きになり，ホームステイ中，毎朝食べていました。

食わず嫌いをせずに何でもトライしてみませんか。日本の食文化は古い歴史があり，むかしの人の生活の知恵でいろいろ工夫されているのです。日本には四季があり，その季節ごとに旬の味もあります。日本の味覚を体験してはじめて，日本を知ることにもなります。

Could I have some more, please?

Use when you want more food or other things.

Dialog

F **Could I have some more of this, please?**

J **Do you like *yakitori*?**

F **Yes, I'll have another cup of sake as well.**

J **Here you are. Sorry to have kept you waiting.**

Why don't you try everything?

There is a food called *nattō* that Japanese people eat frequently. Some Japanese don't like it and many foreigners don't like to eat it either. *Nattō* is fermented soy beans and it's a great health food. Some foreigners say "Soy beans? 100 years old?" and frown on seeing *Nattō*. But one foreigner had one mouthful of *Nattō* and liked it so much that during his home-stay, he ate it every day.

Why not try something new ——don't be put off by its strangeness. Japanese dietary culture has a very long history. Many foods and their preparation have come down to us from our ancestors. The Japanese four seasons are very clearly distinguished and there are special foods for each season. These foods should be eaten and appreciated in their season, referred to as *shun* in Japanese. If you try Japanese food, it will be one way of getting to know the Japanese.

もうおなかいっぱいです。

Mō onaka ippai desu.

食事(しょくじ)がすんで満腹(まんぷく)になったときに言(い)います。

ダイアローグ

F　今日(きょう)はごちそうさまでした。
Kyō wa gochisōsama deshita.

J　どういたしまして。
Dō itashimashite.

F　もうおなかいっぱいです。
Mō onaka ippai desu.

J　では，そろそろ帰(かえ)りましょうか。
Dewa, soro soro kaerimashō ka.

日本(にほん)の飲(の)み物(もの)いろいろ

カルピスという飲(の)み物(もの)をご存知(ぞんじ)ですか。はじめてこれを飲(の)んだ外国人はだれでも「おいしい」といいます。乳酸菌(にゅうさんきん)で作られたものです。これが「初恋(はつこい)の味(あじ)」だといわれると「え？」と首(くび)をかしげる人もいますが，とにかくおいしいことは確(たし)かです。

日本のビールも外国人に評判(ひょうばん)がよいようです。ビールといえばドイツのミュンヘン，アメリカのミルウォーキー，そして日本のサッポロでしたが，いまでは日本の各(かく)ビール会社がさまざまな銘柄(めいがら)のビールを作り，味(あじ)を競(きそ)っています。テレビの宣伝(せんでん)もさかんです。

日本茶(ちゃ)にたくさんの種類(しゅるい)があるのはご存知(ぞんじ)ですか。玉露(ぎょくろ)・煎茶(せんちゃ)・番茶(ばんちゃ)・ほうじ茶(ちゃ)・茎茶(くきちゃ)・玄米茶(げんまいちゃ)など，みんな味がちがいます。

I've had enough, thank you.

Use after dinner when you have had enough to eat.

Dialog

F **Thank you very much for dinner today.**

J **You're welcome.**

F **I've had enough, thank you.**

J **Shall we go then?**

Beverages in Japan

Do you know a drink called '*Calpis*'? Most foreign people come to like the taste of it from the first time they drink it and say "It's delicious." It's made from lactic acid bacillus. The manufacturer says that Calpis is 'the reminder of the taste of first love' but foreigners can't figure out why people call it 'the taste of first lovef. However, it is nice and delicious.

Japanese beer is quite popular among foreigners. When you think about beer, you think of Munich in Germany, Milwaukee in the U.S.A., and *Sapporo* in Hokkaidō. They are well known for their beer. Japanese beer companies are making different brands of beer in competition with each other for the taste, as well as the advertisements on TV.

Do you know that there are various kinds of Japanese tea? There are gyokuro, sencha, bancha, hōjicha, kukicha, genmaicha and so on. They all taste different.

料理の用語　Specific Vocabulary for Cooking

てんぷら，さしみ，すきやき等などは日本語だけで分かります。調理に必要な日本語も覚えておきましょう。

By saying the names of Japanese dishes, such as tenpura, sashimi, sukiyaki and so on in Japanese, you will be more readily understood and so things will be easier for everybody. As well, why not learn these cooking terms?

●調理の動作　Cooking actions

混ぜる　**mix**

かきまわす　**stir**

おろす　**grate**

注ぐ　**pour**

（缶を）開ける　**open**

皮をむく　**peel**

刻む　**carve**

みじん切ぎり　**mince**

（玉子を）割る　**break**

泡立てる　**beat**

切る　**cut**（薄く切る **slice**）

千切り　**long thin strips**

強く切る　**chop**

蒸す　**steam**

煮る　**boil**

焼く　**bake**（こんがり）**broil**（熱く）

揚げる（油で）　**fry**

●調味料　Seasonings

しょう油　**soy sauce**

塩　**salt**

酢　**vinegar**

油　**oil**

ソース　**sauce**

小麦粉　**wheat flour**

パン粉　**bread flour**

●調理用具　Kitchen utensils

フライパン　**frying pan**

煮なべ　**saucepan**

深いなべ　**pot**

ふた　**lid**

せいろ　**steamer**

缶切り　**can opener**

せん抜き　**bottle opener**

湯わかし　**kettle**

なべつかみ　**pot holder**

まな板　**cutting board**

包丁　**kitchen knife**

●その他　Others

電子レンジ　**microwave oven**

ガス台　**burner**

オーブン　**oven**

ミキサー　**blender**

VII

つきあい
Association

ごめんください。

Gomen kudasai.

家を訪問したときに言います。

ダイアローグ

F　ごめんください。
Gomen kudasai.

J　あら，ドロシー，いらっしゃい。
Ara, Doroshi, irasshai.

F　おじゃまします。
Ojama shimasu.

J　さあさあ，どうぞお上がりください。
Sā sā, dōzo oagari kudasai.

日本の家庭を訪問してみたい

日本人は親しくなっても，なかなか自分の家に呼んでくれません。日本人同士でも学生時代ならともかく，おとなになると外だけのつきあいが多くなります。ましてや，外国人にはいい格好をしたい日本人ですから，自分のありのままの生活は見せたくないと思うのがふつうです。

しかし，中には外国人に対しオープンな心をもった日本人もいます。「いちど日本の家庭を見てみたい」と言えば，「じゃ，こんどの日曜にいらっしゃい」と招かれるかもしれません。

訪問するときは，約束の時間を守ること。そしてちょっとしたおみやげをもっていくのもちょっとした心遣いです。きっと喜ばれます。

国の家族写真をもっていくと話題が広がるでしょう。

Hello.

When you visit a home, say this.

Dialog

F **Hello.**

J **Oh, Dorothy, hello.**

F **May I come in?**

J **Yes, please do.**

Visiting a Japanese family is desirable.

The Japanese don't invite people to their homes readily even though you may have become friendly with them. Even the Japanese themselves usually associate outside their homes, except for schoolchildren, who visit one another at home. Moreover, Japanese want to be seen at their best, so they don't want to reveal their life as it really is.

But among Japanese people there are many who are openhearted. So if you tell them "I'd like to see a Japanese home at least once.", they will probably say "Well, please come to my house. Is next Sunday all right?"

When you visit a home, you should be punctual. Bringing inexpensive and small gifts is considerate. Your host will be delighted.

If you bring photographs of your family, conversation should flow easily from this starting topic.

どうぞ。どうも。

Dō zo. Dō mo.

よく使われる簡単で，ていねいな日本語です。

ダイアローグ

J　お先にどうぞ。
　　Osaki ni dōzo.

F　あ，どうも。
　　A, dōmo.

J　さあ，お茶をどうぞ。
　　Sā, ocha o dōzo.

F　どうも，ありがとうございます。
　　Dō mo, arigatō gozaimasu.

「どうぞ」「どうも」で十分通じます

「どうぞ」「どうも」で通じる状況はいろいろあります。

J：どうぞ。(家にお入りください)　F：どうも。
J：どうぞ。(部屋にお上がりください)　F：どうも。
J：どうぞ。(いすにおかけください)　F：どうも。
J：どうぞ。(ジュースを)　F：どうも。
J：どうぞ。(食事をめしあがれ)　F：どうも。
J：どうぞ。(お先に)　F：どうも。

「さあ，どうぞ」は親しみがこもった言いかたになります。それに対し，「あ，どうも」は受け手のほうがやや恐縮した感じになります。日本人の好きな受け答えのひとつです。

Please. Thank you.

Frequently used in simple and polite Japanese.

Dialog

J **After you.**

F **Thank you.**

J **Have a cup of tea.**

F **Thank you very much.**

"*Dōzo*", "*Dōmo*" is enough to communicate your thanks.

There are many occasions that we can communicate using "*Dōzo*" and "*Dōmo*".

J: *Dōzo*. (Please come into my house.) F: *Dōmo*.
J: *Dōzo*. (Please come into my house.) F: *Dōmo*.
J: *Dōzo*. (Please come into my room.) F: *Dōmo*.
J: *Dōzo*. (Please sit down.) F: *Dōmo*.
J: *Dōzo*. (Have a glass of juice.) F: *Dōmo*.
J: *Dōzo*. (Please have dinner.) F: *Dōmo*.
J: *Dōzo*. (After you.) F: *Dōmo*.

"*Sā, dōzo*" is quite a friendly expression. "*A, dōmo*" is used when the speaker is feeling under some obligation and wants to express a particular courtesy. This is one of Japanese people's favorite responses.

いただきます。

Itadaki masu.

食事の前や人にごちそうになるときに言います。

ダイアローグ

J　どうぞ，めしあがってください。
Dō zo, meshi agatte kudasai.

F　では，いただきます。
Dewa, itadaki masu.

J　おはしは使えますか。
Ohashi wa tsukaemasu ka?

F　はい，だいじょうぶです。
Hai, daijōbu desu.

「いただきます」「ごちそうさま」

食事の前後に言う感謝のあいさつです。だれに感謝するかというと，食事をすることができる神への感謝，食事をつくってくれた人への感謝，食事の材料を生産してくれた人たちへの感謝，時にはレストランなどでごちそうしてくれる人への感謝を表すことばです。

日本人は，はしだけで食事をします。外国人と異なる点は，茶わんやおわんを手にもって食事をすることです。はしだけで食事がしにくいときは遠慮なく，ナイフやフォーク，スプーンをもらってください。大豆をはしでひとつずつ取って手ぎわよく別の入れ物ものに移せたらあなたはもう本物の日本人です。

Itadakimasu. (Bon appétit!/Enjoy your food!)

Use before starting to eat or when someone treats you.

Dialog

J **Please have some.**

F **Itadakimasu.**

J **Can you use chopsticks?**

F **Yes, it's alright.**

"*Itadakimasu*", "*Gochisōsama*"

There are expressions of gratitude which we say before and after a meal. We are expressing gratitude to the gods, the person who cooked the dinner and the people who produced the ingredients for the dinner, and sometimes towards a person who has treated us at a restaurant.

We use chopsticks when we eat. Another point which differs from foreign cultures is that we pick up our bowls with our hands. When you find it difficult to eat with chopsticks, don't hesitate to request a knife and fork. When you can move soy beans with chopsticks quickly from one bowl to another, you are on your way to becoming a real Japanese.

もう，けっこうです。

Mō, kekkō desu.

相手のサービスに十分満足し，それ以上は断わるときに言います。

ダイアローグ

J　コーヒー，もういっぱい，いかがですか。
Kōhi, mō ippai, ikaga desu ka?

F　もう，けっこうです。
Mō, kekkō desu.

J　では，アイスクリームは。
Dewa, aisukurimu wa?

F　あ，いただきます。大好きです。
A, itadakimasu. Daisuki desu.

「もう，けっこうです」は便利なことば

もともと日本人は親切な国民性ですから，その習性がエスカレートし，サービスを強制する人がときどきいます。サービスを中断したり，もてなしが中途半端では失礼だと思うからです。そういう時の「もう，けっこうです」はたいへん便利な表現です。ぜひ覚えておいてください。

外国人と親しくなるのをたいへん喜ぶ日本人はたくさんいます。すこしことばが通じたり，気が合ったりするととても親切にしてくれます。人によっては，物をやたらにくれる人もいます。物をもらってもお返しの必要はありません。

I have had enough, thank you.

For use when you are satisfied and wish to decline your host's offer.

Dialog

J **What about another cup of coffee?**

F **No, thank you. I have had enough.**

J **What about ice cream then?**

F **Yes, please. I really enjoy ice cream.**

"*Mō, kekkō desu.*" is a convenient phrase.

In their effort to be hospitable, Japanese hosts can sometimes overdo things. The phrase, "*Mō, kekkō desu.*" (I've had enough.) is a convenient expression when you want to turn something down, so it should be committed to memory and used when necessary.

There are many Japanese who enjoy the company and friendship of foreigners. They can be very kind and helpful and often present their foreign friends with gifts of various sorts. But don't feel that you need to give a gift to your friends in return.

わー，うれしい。

Wā, ureshii.

同意して喜びを表すときに言います。

ダイアローグ

J　ねえ，マイク，お祭りにいかない。
Nē, Maiku, omatsuri ni ikanai?

F　それは，おもしろそう。
Sorewa, omoshirosō.

J　おみこし，かつぐ。
Omikoshi, katsugu?

F　わー，うれしい。
Wā, ureshii.

町内会の人とつきあおう

日本の地域社会は教会活動のようなつきあいはありませんが，共同で行う道路の清掃や，神社のお祭り，お寺の盆踊りといった行事にはみんなが参加します。こういうチャンスにはぜひ参加しましょう。近隣の人とのつきあいから何か新しいことが生まれるかもしれません。

あなたは日本の銭湯に行く勇気がありますか。日本にかぎらず東アジアの国々では銭湯から地域の人たちとの交流が生まれます。「裸のつきあい」という表現は，心を開いた人間関係のことを言います。「お殿様でも家来でも，お風呂に入るときは，みんなはだか」というむかしの歌もあります。人間みんな同じ，という考えかたなのです。

Wā, ureshii! (Oh, I am pleased!/That's great!)

Use when you agree with something and to express joy.

Dialog

J Mike, shall we go to the Japanese festival?

F That sounds interesting.

J Would you like to help carry a portable shrine?

F *Wā, ureshii!* (Oh, I'm so pleased!, or That's great!)

Associate with the people living in the same neighborhood.

The Japanese neighborhood community is not like a church community, but its members all take part in activities such as cleaning public roads together and celebrating the local shrine's festival or Bon Odori. Do join in these kinds of activities. You are bound to get new insights into Japanese life and culture from them and to make some good friends.

Do you have the courage to go to a Japanese public bath? Not only in Japan, but in other east Asian countries, a feeling of community with people living in the same neighborhood is strengthened in the public baths.

We have an expression 'naked association'. It refers to a relationship with a warm-hearted person. We have an old song, which goes like this "A king or retainer, they are all naked when they have a bath." It makes us feel that we are all equal, just human beings together.

おじゃましました。

Ojama shimashita.

訪問先から去るときのあいさつです。

ダイアローグ

F　そろそろ，しつれいします。
Soro soro, shitsurei shimasu.

J　そうですか。それは，それは。
Sō desu ka. Sorewa, sorewa.

F　どうも，おじゃましました。
Dō mo, ojama shimashita.

J　いいえ，どういたしまして。
Iie, dō itashi mashite.

日本人の移動の時期

日本では，みんながいっせいに休暇をとったり，移動したりすることが多く，その時期は，どこも人でいっぱいになります。

年末年始は故郷へ帰る人たちで，交通機関はたいへん混雑します。正月3が日は有名な神社に初もうでの人が殺到します。ゴールデンウィークには道路も新幹線も飛行機も大混雑です。夏休みも休暇で移動する人が多いのですが，特にお盆の時期はピークになります。

Ojama shimashita. (Thank you very much./I am afraid I've taken up too much of your time.)

Saying good-bye when you leave a host's house.

Dialog

F I must be off now.

J Do you have to go? Well, well.

F *Dōmo, ojama shimashita.* (Thank you very much.)

J Not at all.

The periods when Japanese people take a trip

At certain times of the year, almost all Japanese take their holidays and like to return to their hometown in great crowds. That causes terrible traffic jams everywhere.

At the year-end and new year days, travel routes all over Japan are filled with people who want to make a visit home. During the three days of the new year holiday, millions of people gather at famous temples and shrines to pay their respects. At the beginning of May there is Golden Week. Huge crowds of people flood the roads, thet rains, the *Shinkansen* and the airports. Summer holidays are the time when many people tend to move around, but especially *Obon* (the Festival for the Dead) is ranked as the peak of crowdedness.

では，お元気で。

Dewa, ogenki de.

親しい間柄のていねいな別れのあいさつです。

ダイアローグ

J　また，いらしてください。
Mata, irashite kudasai.

F　ではみなさん，お元気で。
Dewa minasan, ogenki de.

J　カレンさんにも，よろしく。
Karen-san nimo, yoroshiku.

F　はい，お伝えします。
Hai, otsutae shimasu.

ホームステイができれば最高

日本人家族と親しい間柄になれば，週末を利用しての1泊か2泊のホームステイが経験できるかもしれません。

ホームステイは，家族の一員として過ごすひとときになります。日本人の生活様式のすべてがわかるでしょう。お互いにおとなですから，できるだけ自分の国の文化や習慣についての意見交換をしましょう。政治や宗教の議論よりむしろ，ふつうの生活の中から相違を発見しお互いの理解を深めることがたいせつです。

お客さまではありませんから，食事の仕度，掃除・洗濯も手伝いましょう。ひとつひとつの活動から日本語を覚えることができるでしょう。

Take care of yourselves.

Saying farewell in a polite way to close friends.

Dialog

J Please come again.

F Take care of yourselves.

J Give my regards to Karen.

F Yes, I will.

Your best opportunity might be when you can experience a homestay.

If you become very friendly with a Japanese family, you might be invited to spend one or two nights at their house on the weekend.

During your homestay, you would come to stay in a Japanese family as a member of the family. And you can learn all about the Japanese life style. As adults, we can exchange information about the culture and customs of our own countries. It is important that we should refrain from discussing controversial topics such as politics or religion, and concentrate on the interesting differences in ordinary life, and so understand one another better.

You are not considered to be a guest but rather a family member, so help in preparing dinner, and cleaning and washing. You will learn Japanese from each activity.

日本人の名字と名前　Family names and given names of Japanese

名字：日本人の名字はおよそ30,000 あるといわれます。その中で特にポピュラーなものを 20 選びました。

Family names: There are approximately 30,000 different Japanese family names. Twenty particularly common family names are listed below.

伊藤	小林	田中	松本	山口
上田	佐藤	千葉	村上	山田
加藤	鈴木	中村	森	吉田
木村	高橋	林	山本	渡辺

名前：名前は時代によって流行があります。年号がかわったときや，有名人の結婚・出産などがあったときなどに，特に顕著です。女性の名前はひらがなだけのものもあります。最近流行の名前を中心に男女 10 ずつ選びました。

Given Names: Trends in the choice of babies' names differ with each decade. Characteristically, Japanese parents tend to name their children after famous people, who were married or had a child around the same time as they had their baby. Often some girls' names are written only in hiragana.

Below are listed the ten most popular Japanese boys' names and the ten most popular Japanese girls' names.

男	諒太	拓也	浩平	直人	淳一
(Boy)	裕介	明宏	修	英樹	慎太郎
女	しおり	麻衣子	茜	由香	沙織
(Girl)	なつみ	美穂	あおい	理佐	ちひろ

VIII

日本を知る
Getting to know Japan

歌舞伎を見にいきました。

Kabuki o mini ikimashita.

歌舞伎は日本の伝統的な演劇の1つとしてとくに有名です。

ダイアローグ

F　きのう，歌舞伎を見にいきました。
Kinō, Kabuki o mini ikimashita.

J　どうでしたか。
Dō deshita ka.

F　ええ，とてもファンタスティック。
Ee, totemo fantasutikku.

J　そう，たしかに幻想的ね。
Sō, tashikani gensōteki ne.

日本特有の民衆劇・歌舞伎

日本に来た外国人はだれでもいちどは歌舞伎を見たいと言います。それほど日本独特の演劇なのです。

歌舞伎は1か月ごとの出し物で，1日2回の公演です。歌舞伎の真髄を知るには少なくとも1年はかかるでしょう。

歌舞伎座には一幕見という，短時間で安く見る方法があります。舞台から遠い天井桟敷ですが，それでも歌舞伎の一端はわかります。せりふや解説などイヤホーンを使えば英語の説明が聞けます。

I went to see *Kabuki*.

Kabuki is a famous Japanese theatrical performance with a long history.

Dialog

F **I went to see *Kabuki* yesterday.**

J **Did you understand it?**

F **Yes, it was fantastic!**

J **Yes, it is fantastic, isn't it?**

Kabuki: Japanese popular traditional theater performance

Every foreigner who visits Japan says that they want to see *Kabuki* once. Kabuki is Japan's traditional theater and has great appeal for foreigners.

The *Kabuki* program changes every month. There are 2 performances a day. It takes a year to understand *Kabuki*'s spirit.

In *Kabuki-za*, there is a way to see Kabuki cheaply called '*Hitomakumi*' in which you can watch it for just a short time. Although you get a seat in the upper gallery which is far from the stage and watch it from there, it is possible to see quite well. And if you use earphones, you can hear the dialog or explanations in English.

日本は美しい国ですね。

Nihon wa utsukushii kuni desu ne.

日本の印象を聞かれる機会は多いはず。

ダイアローグ

J　日本に来て，どう思いましたか。
Nihon ni kite,　dō　omoi　mashita ka.

F　日本は美しい国ですね。
Nihon wa utsukushii kuni desu ne.

J　どんなところが。
Donna　tokoroga?

F　みどりがきれいです。
Midori　ga kirei　desu.

四季を通して雨量が多い

日本は4つの大きな島と無数の小島から成っています。北海道・本州・四国・九州からさらに南の沖縄諸島まで南北におよそ4,000kmの温帯圏にあり，1年を通し四季の変化があります。四季を通して雨量が多いのも日本の特徴です。4島それぞれ高い山があり，降った雨は急傾斜の河を一気に下り海に注ぎます。また山肌に浸みた水は樹木を潤し，わき水となって作物を育てます。

雨上がりの緑は生気をとりもどし一段と美しくなります。また，冬が過ぎ，木の芽がふきはじめる春先には，あちこちの山に淡い緑が安らぎを与えてくれます。さらに田植えがすんで夏が近づくと，米作地帯では広大な緑のじゅうたんになるのです。

Japan is a beautiful country, isn't it?

There must be many opportunities where you would be asked what you think about Japan.

Dialog

J What do you think of Japan?

F Japan is a beautiful country, isn't it?

J What do you find beautiful?

F Natural areas in Japan are beautiful.

There is a lot of rain throughout the four seasons.

Japan consists of four big islands and innumerable small islands: Hokkaido, Honshu, Shikoku, Kyushu and the more southern Okinawa islands. From north to south it runs for 4,000 km. It is located in the temperate zone and there are four seasonal changes in a year. Japan characteristically has a lot of rain throughout all four seasons. Each of the four big islands has high mountains. The falling rain dashes down their steep sides into the rivers and flows into the sea. The water soaks into the surface of mountains, and waters trees and freshens springs.

After the rain, the vegetation looks shiny and regains its vigor. With the passing of winter comes the early spring. The mountain trees bring out their buds and their light green color, here and there, which gives us a feeling of tranquility. When rice planting is finished, the summer approaches and the rice-growing areas become a vast green carpet.

おめでとうございます。

Omedetō gozai masu.

新年，結婚式，誕生日などにかわすお祝いのあいさつです。

ダイアローグ

F　本日は，おめでとうございます。
　Honjitsu wa, omedetō gozai masu.

J　花嫁さんの着物，どう。
　Hanayome-san no kimono, dō?

F　きれいな白。白いヘッドバンドも。
　Kireina shiro. Shiroi heddobando mo.

J　あら，あれは「角隠し」よ。
　Ara, are wa „Tsuno-Kakushi“ yo.

もしも結婚式に招待されたら

最近，結婚式の出席者の中に外国人の姿をよく見かけます。もしも，あなたが招待状をもらったらどうしますか。

招待状は二つ折りの案内状と，返信用のはがき，会場の地図が入っています。スケジュールを確認し，すぐに出席の返信を送りましょう。当日の結婚式は神式であれば親戚しか参加できませんが，キリスト教式ならだれでも参列できます。つづいて披露宴になりますが，入口の受付でみんながお祝い金を出します。市販のお祝い用ののし袋にお金（パーティー費用相当）を入れ，表の下に自分の名前を書いて持っていくのが習慣です。服装は男性なら黒の上下に白いタイ，女性はドレッシーであれば個性に応じ何でもかまいません。

Congratulations.

Expressions used when celebrating New Year's Day, weddings, birthdays and so on.

Dialog

F **Congratulations.**

J **What do you think of the bride in her wedding kimono?**

F **That's a beautiful white kimono. The bride's hood, too.**

J **Oh, that is 'Tsunokakushi'.**

You may be invited to a wedding ceremony.

Recently a number of foreigners have been invited to various Japanese wedding ceremonies. What should you do if you receive a wedding invitation?

Invitations consist of a card folded in two, a reply card and a map of the wedding hall. Confirm the schedule and send back the reply card promptly. If the wedding service is to be held according to Shinto rites, only relatives can participate, but if it's to be held according to Christian rites, anybody can participate. After the ceremony, there will be a reception. At the entrance to the reception we all give congratulatory money. It is our custom that we put the money into paper envelopes made specially for the occasion. They are sold at many shops. We write our name in the space provided in the lower part of the envelope. Men should wear dark or formal suits, with a white tie, and women should wear a formal dress appropriate to their age and situation.

ううん，あんまり。

Uun, anmari.

乗り気でないときの返事です。

ダイアローグ

J　日本のお能，好き。
Nihon no o-noh, suki?

F　ううん，あんまり。
Uun, anmari.

J　どうして。
Dōshite?

F　だって，へんな声だから。
Datte, henna koe dakara.

日本の「わび」と「さび」

外国の人に，本当の日本の感覚をわかってもらうには，「わび」と「さび」の心を知る必要があるでしょう。いずれのことばも簡単に言えば「静かな様子」といったところです。茶道や俳句（世界でいちばん短い詩）でいう「わび」はまさに静けさを楽しむという意味です。「さび」とは，静けさがさらに洗練され，純芸術化されたものをいいます。

雑念があっては，茶道も生花もできません。どうやって静の世界に入り込んでいけるかなのです。だからといってそれは宗教ではありません。日本を知る意味で，いちどその境地に浸ってみませんか。

Not very much.

An answer when you don't feel positive about something.

Dialog

J	**Do you like Japan's Noh play?**
F	**Not very much.**
J	**Why?**
F	**Because they speak with strange voices.**

Japan's '*Wabi*', and '*Sabi*'

To understand Japan's real essence foreigners must understand the concept of '*wabi*', and '*sabi*'. The simplest meaning for both words is a quiet state. '*Wabi*' in tea ceremony or in *haiku* (the shortest verse in the world) means the enjoyment of tranquility. '*Sabi*' expresses the tranquility and elegant simplicity which is found in sophisticated art forms.

One can not perform tea ceremony or design flower arrangements while they are thinking about earthly things. The problem is how we can attain a tranquil state of mind. But the concept of '*sabi*' is not religious. Why don't you try to experience this state in order to understand Japan?

あー，びっくりした。

Ah, bikkuri shita.

驚いたときに言います。

ダイアローグ

J　わっ。
Wa!

F　あー，びっくりした。それ，なに。
Ah, bikkuri shita. Sore, nani?

J　驚いた。能のお面だよ。
Odoroita? Noh no omen dayo.

F　ああ，そう。
Ah, sō.

日本の葬式とお墓

日本では人が死ぬと，通常2日間の葬儀を行います。最初はお通夜が行われます。友人・知人が弔問に訪れます。その夜は親類が集まって夜通し死者を見守ります。その翌日は告別式が行われ，ふたたび友人・知人が弔問に訪れます。それが終わると死者を霊きゅう車に乗せ，親しい人といっしょに火葬場へ行きます。死者が火葬されると，二人一組で骨をはしではさみ骨つぼに入れ儀式が終わります。

死者は死後7日から49日の間，魂がこの世にさまよったあと，あの世に旅立つといわれています。そのあとお墓に骨を埋めるのです。祭典は死後1年，3年，7年，13年，33年とつづいて行われます。毎年春と秋，お墓参りに行き花束と線香を供えます。

Ā bikkuri-shita. (You gave me such a surprise!)

For use when you are surprised.

Dialog

J **Wah!**

F ***Ā bikkuri-shita.*** **(You gave me such a surprise!) What is this?**

J **You are surprised? This is a Noh mask.**

F **Oh, I see.**

Japanese funerals and graves

In Japan, if someone dies, we usually take 2 days for the funeral. We have a vigil first. Friends and acquaintances call to express their condolences. Relatives sit the night out with the deceased. The next day, a farewell service is held, and friends and acquaintances visit again. After that, the deceased is carried into the hearse to go to the crematorium with close relatives and friends.

After the deceased has been cremated, the bones will be put into a special urn with chopsticks held by two of the mourners and the funeral rites finish.

During the 7 to 49 days after death, the soul of the deceased wanders around this world, and then journeys to the next world. After that, the bones will be buried in a grave. Memorial services for the dead are held continuously, at 1 year, 3 years, 7 years, 13 years, . . . until 33 years after the death. We go to graves in spring and autumn every year and offer flowers and sticks of incense.

とってもかわいい。

Tottemo kawaii.

小(ちい)さく愛(あい)らしい子(こ)どもや小物(こもの)にたいして言(い)います。

ダイアローグ

F　あの子(こ)，とってもかわいい。
Ano ko, tottemo kawaii.

J　テレビのコマーシャルの子(こ)。
Terebi no komāsyaru no ko?

F　そう，お人形(にんぎょう)みたい。
Sō, oningyō mitai.

J　ほんとに。
Honto-ni.

テレビ番組(ばんぐみ)

ことばがわからないとテレビをみてもおもしろくないですね。衛星(えいせい)放送(ほうそう)受信機(じゅしんき)のあるテレビなら英語(えいご)のニュースを聞(き)くことができます。番組(ばんぐみ)によっては英日(えいにち)の2か国語(こくご)放送(ほうそう)をやっています。

相撲(すもう)放送(ほうそう)をみたことがありますか。最近(さいきん)は外国人(がいこくじん)力士(りきし)が活躍(かつやく)しています。スポーツ番組(ばんぐみ)も国際化(こくさいか)しています。サッカー，ゴルフ，野球(やきゅう)，スキー，バスケット，柔道(じゅうどう)など各国(かっこく)の選手(せんしゅ)が登場(とうじょう)します。

日本の時代劇(じだいげき)はみましたか。さむらいがひとりで大(おお)ぜいの悪者(わるもの)をやっつけるのは痛快(つうかい)です。

コマーシャルは，日本の生活(せいかつ)を知(し)る意味(いみ)で役立(やくだ)ちます。いろいろなコマーシャルがありますが，現在(げんざい)の日本のセンスを見(み)ることができます。

Really sweet.

To use when you praise small children or receive a small present and so on.

Dialog

F **That girl is really sweet.**

J **The girl in the TV commercial?**

F **Yes. She's like a doll.**

J **Yes, really.**

TV Programs

If you don't understand the language, it's no fun to watch television. You can hear English news if you have a TV with a satellite broadcast receiver. Some programs are broadcast in both English and Japanese.

Have you seen a *sumō* match? Foreign *sumō* wrestlers have become very successful these days. We can watch foreign athletes on TV. Foreigners often appear in football, golf, baseball, skiing, basketball, *jūdō* and so on.

Have you seen a Japanese period drama? It is exciting to see a *samurai* —— like a superman —— beat up the villains.

Watching TV commercials will help you to understand Japanese life. There are many kinds of commercials, so you can see the humor of contemporary Japan.

なぜ。

Naze?

理由(りゆう)を聞(き)くときに言(い)います。

ダイアローグ

J　さあ，もう行(い)かなくちゃ。
Sā, mō ikanakucha.

F　なぜ。
Naze?

J　3時(じ)に約束(やくそく)がある。
San-ji ni yakusoku ga aru.

F　いそがしいね。
Isogashii ne.

日本(にほん)のビジネスマンの生活(せいかつ)

アジアのある国(くに)の経営評論家(けいえいひょうろんか)が，自国(じこく)と日本の会社員(かいしゃいん)の比較(ひかく)をしてこう言(い)いました。「うちの国(くに)の社員(しゃいん)は 5 時(じ)退社前(たいしゃまえ)に帰(かえ)りじたくをし 5 時(じ)キッカリに帰(かえ)るが，日本の社員(しゃいん)は 5 時(じ)までに仕事(しごと)が終(お)わらなければ，それが終(お)わるまでやって，それから帰(かえ)りじたくをする。その時間差(じかんさ)が 1 年(ねん)，5 年，10 年経(た)てば膨大(ぼうだい)になりそれだけ水(みず)をあけられる」と。これはたしかにそうかもしれません。

日本人は家庭(かてい)もだいじにしますが，会社優先人間(かいしゃゆうせんにんげん)が多(おお)いのも事実(じじつ)です。必要(ひつよう)なら残業(ざんぎょう)もやり，休日(きゅうじつ)をはさんで出張(しゅっちょう)もします。長期単身赴任(ちょうきたんしんふにん)で頑張(がんば)っているお父(とう)さんもたくさんいます。

Why?

Use when you want to know the reason for something.

Dialog

J **Well, I must be going now.**

F **Why?**

J **I have an appointment at 3 o'clock.**

F **You are so busy.**

The life of a Japanese businessman

Some Asian management critics make statements comparing the employees of his own country wit hJapanese employees, and say "Employees in our country get ready to leave the office before 5 o'clock and leave just at 5 o'clock. But if a Japanese employee couldn't finish his work by 5 o'clock, he would finish it first and then prepare to leave. If this difference in working time becomes bigger and bigger with the length of service, five or ten years later we would notice that the total number of working hours make a Japanese company progress farther eventually." This may be true.

Many Japanese think a great deal of their families, but there is another principle that many Japanese people believe in that their business matters come first. They work overtime if necessary. They go on business trips even on weekends. Many fathers who have to live apart from their families because of business for a long time endure a lonesome life.

それで，どうしたの。

Sorede, dōshita no?

話の先を聞きたいときに言います。

ダイアローグ

J　きょう，合気道場へ行ってね。
　　Kyō,　aikidōjō　e　itte ne.

F　それで，どうしたの。
　　Sorede,　dōshita no?

J　ついに，入門したよ。
　　Tsuini,　nyūmon shita yo.

F　ぼくも，やりたいな。
　　Boku mo,　yaritai na.

人気がある日本の武道

日本の武道は外国人男性に人気があります。日本の柔道はすでに世界的なスポーツになりましたが，やはり本家の日本でじっくり学びたいと思う人が多いようです。

合気道もなかなかの人気です。黒帯をもらうまで自国には帰らないと頑張っている人もいます。

空手はもともと沖縄から伝わってきたものですが，武器をもたずに身を守る技として女性にもやる人が増えています。

そのほかに，剣道は防具をつけ竹刀をもってする武道です。また日本の弓道は西洋のアーチェリーと違って，武道としての精神統一が要求されます。

Then, what will happen next?

Use these words when you want to know what happens next.

Dialog

J **Today I went to the training center of *aikidō*.**

F **Then what will happen next?**

J **Finally, I decided to join in *aikidō* training course.**

F **I'd like to join, too.**

The popular Japanese martial arts

Japanese martial arts are popular among foreign men. Japanese *jūdō* has become one of the world-famous sports nowadays. However, there are some people who want to learn it in Japan because *jūdō* originated in Japan.

Many men like *aikidō* and positive trainees sometimes say " I won't return to my own country till I get the black belt."

Karate originally came from Okinawa and it does not require any weapons when fighting. Thus, the number of women who practice karate as a means of protecting themselves is growing rapidly.

As well, *kendō* is a martial art in which a trainee should wear *bōgu* (armor) and play it with shinai (bamboo sword) in his hands. In comparison with Western archery, Japanese archery requires a great deal of mental discipline.

日本の祝祭日　Japanese Holidays

日本には公の祝祭日が，15 あります。

We have 15 annual national holidays in Japan.

1月1日	元日	Jan. 1	1New Year’s Day
1月第2月曜日	成人の日	Second Monday of January	
			Coming of Age Day
2月11日	建国記念の日	Feb. 11	11National Foundation Day
3月21日	春分の日	Mar. 21	Vernal Equinox Day
4月29日	みどりの日	Apr. 29	Greenery Day
5月3日	憲法記念日	May. 3	Constitution Memorial Day
5月4日	国民の祝日	May. 4	National Holiday
5月5日	こどもの日	May. 5	Children’s Day
7月20日	海の日	uly. 20	Marine Day
9月15日	敬老の日	Sep. 15	Respect-for-the-Aged Day
9月23日	秋分の日	Sep. 23	Autumnal Equinox Day
10月第2月曜日	体育の日	Second Monday of October	
			Health-Sports Day
11月3日	文化の日	Nov. 3	Culture Day
11月23日	勤労感謝の日	Nov. 23	Labor Thanksgiving Day
12月23日	天皇誕生日	Dec. 23	The Emperor's Birthday

IX

トラブル
Troubles

あれー，どうしよう。

Arē, dōshiyō.

困ったことがおき，自分ではどうしたらよいかわからないときに言います。

ダイアローグ

F　あれー，どうしよう。
Arē, dōshiyō.

J　どうしたの。
Dōshita no?

F　電車の中に，忘れた。
Densha no naka ni, wasureta!

J　なにを。
Nani o?

電車・バス・タクシーの忘れ物

人はよく忘れ物をします。乗り物のほか公衆電話，公衆トイレ，レストラン，さらにどこに忘れたかもわからない場合もあります。

乗り物の場合は，降りた駅の遺失物係へ行きます。タクシーの場合，おそらくだれも会社名をおぼえていませんから，地域のタクシー遺失物係に問い合わせます。

公共の場所での忘れ物はまず現場に行ってみて，もしなければすぐ警察に行き遺失物届けを提出します。

忘れ物をしたとき，その時間・場所および物・中身を正確に説明しなければなりませんから，どうしても日本人の助けがいるでしょう。届け出が早いほど手元に戻る確率が高くなります。

Oh, what am I going to do?

Use this when trouble happens and you don't know what to do about it.

Dialog

F **Oh, what am I going to do?**

J **What happened?**

F **I've left something in the train.**

J **What did you forget?**

Lost property in the train, bus and taxi

People often leave things in taxis and public transport, public telephone boxes, public toilets, restaurants and places they don't remember.

If you leave something in a train (bus), you should go to the lost property counter at the station where you got off. If you leave something in a taxi, you will probably not remember the company's name, so contact the lost property department of any taxi company in the area.

If you leave something in a public place, you should go back to that place. If you can't find it, go to the police immediately and report it as lost property.

Probably you will need an interpreter because when you report the loss, you will have to tell the officers about the time, place, and things which you lost. If you report the loss immediately, you will have a better chance of getting your things back.

ここが痛いんです。

Koko ga itain desu.

からだの痛い個所を示して言います。

ダイアローグ

F　ここが痛いんです。
　　Koko ga itain desu.
J　胃だね，きっと。
　　I dane, kitto.
F　くすり，ありますか。
　　Kusuri, arimasu ka?
J　それより，医者に行こう。
　　Soreyori, isha ni ikō.

具合の悪い個所は手で示す

具合の悪い個所を日本人に伝えるのは手で押さえて示すのがいちばんです。いちいちからだの部分の名称を日本語で言わなくてもいいからです。

季節のかわり目はかぜを引きやすくなります。ゆっくり寝るのが一番です。もし熱があれば体から汗を出して治す方法もあります。なるべく市販の薬に頼らず，早目に医者にみてもらいましょう。国民健康保険証を忘れずに。

持病のある人（アレルギー，糖尿，高血圧など）はきちんと申告しましょう。

I have a pain here.

Use when you are in pain, point to the place where you feel pain.

Dialog

F **I have a pain here.**

J **Maybe it's your stomach.**

F **Do you have any pills for it?**

J **You had better go to the doctor.**

Indicate the spot where you feel sick or pain with your hand.

The best way to tell a Japanese person that you are feeling sick or in pain is by indicating and touching the spot with your hand. You don't have to say the name of the part in Japanese.

When the season changes, people often get colds. Try to rest then. If you have a temperature, you can sweat away the fever with medicine. If possible, do not depend on patent medicines. You should see a doctor in the early stages of your illness. Do not forget to take your National Health Insurance card with you.

If you have any chronic ailment (an allergy, diabetes, high blood pressure, etc.), you must tell the doctor.

だれか，助けて。

Dareka, tasukete!

緊急のとき，大声で人に助けを求めるときに言います。

ダイアローグ

F　だれか，助けて。
Dareka, tasukete!

J　なにがあったの。
Nani ga attano?

F　財布を盗られた。
Saifu o torareta.

J　すぐ，交番へ行こう。
Sugu, kōban e ikō.

犯罪に遭ったとき

日本は安全な国といわれていますが，それでも時には悪い人がいます。とくに人込みには十分注意しましょう。財布を腰のポケットに入れたり，ハンドバッグを開けたまま持ち歩いてはスリにねらわれます。込んだ電車に乗る女性はチカンにも気をつけましょう。暗い夜道のひとり歩きも危険です。出かけるときはきちんと戸締まりしましょう。どこの国でも自分を守るのは自分です。

もし犯罪に遭ったらすぐ警察に知らせましょう。街中でも郊外でも 110 番をダイヤルすれば来てくれます。ただし，正確に場所を伝えなければいけません。現場に来る方法ではなく，所・番地そして名前です。たとえば「いま，銀座 4 の 1 にいます。ブライアンです」のように。

Help! Somebody.

When it's urgent, call for help in a loud voice.

Dialog

F **Help! Somebody.**

J **What happened?**

F **My wallet has been stolen.**

J **Let's go to the police straight away.**

When you experience trouble.

It is said that Japan is a safe country, but there are some wicked people around. You should be careful, especially in a crowd. You will be noticed if you put your wallet in your hip pocket or walk with your handbag open. Women should be careful of molesters in crowded trains. It can be dangerous to walk alone in the dark street. When you go out, lock your room securely. You have to take precautions in any country.

If you are involved in or witness a crime, report it to the police immediately. If you dial 110, the police will come straight away, either in town or in the suburbs. But you will have to give them the right address. You just tell them the address and your name. Don't worry about giving them directions. For example, you could say "I'm at Ginza 4-*chōme* 1. My name is Brian."

熱があります。

Netsu ga arimasu.

薬局に行き，かぜの症状を話します。

ダイアローグ

F　熱があります。
Netsu ga arimasu.

J　かぜですか。
Kaze desu ka?

F　アスピリンをください。
Asupirin o kudasai.

J　アレルギーはありますか。
Arerugi wa arimasu ka?

いろいろな症状の伝えかた

薬を買うときは，症状を正確に伝えることが大切です。

＜症状＞熱がある，吐き気がする，のどがはれる，食欲がない，せきがでる，肩がこる，手がしびれる，血を吐く，便秘，下痢，足がつる，くしゃみが止まらない，しゃっくり，寒気がする，いびきをかく，化膿する，腰がまがらない，苦しい，めまいがする，たんが出る，鼻水が出る

＜処置＞熱を計る，うがいをする，薬をのむ，よく眠る，氷で冷やす，熱いスープをのむ，肩をもむ，ぬり薬をつける，湿布する

I've got a temperature.

Explain your symptoms to a pharmacy assistant.

Dialog

F **I've got a temperature.**

J **Perhaps you are getting a cold?**

F **May I have an aspirin?**

J **Yes. Do you have any allergies?**

How to describe various symptoms.

It is important to explain your symptoms precisely when you are buying patent medicines.

＜Symptoms＞

Have a temperature, feel sick, have a sore throat, no appetite, have a cough, stiff shoulder, numb hand, vomit blood, constipation, diarrhea, have a cramp, keep sneezing, hiccups, shivering, snoring, festering, impossible to move some part of one's body, difficult to breathe, feel dizzy, have phlegm, a runny nose, etc.

＜Treatment＞

Take one's temperature, gargle, take medicine, sleep well, cool oneself with ice, have hot soup, massage one's shoulders, apply ointment, apply a compress.

いつできますか。

Itsu dekimasu ka?

修理などのできあがる日をたずねるときに言います。

ダイアローグ

F　カメラを修理してください。
　　Kamera o shūri shite kudasai.

J　はい，かしこまりました。
　　Hai, kashikomarimashita.

F　いつできますか。
　　Itsu dekimasu ka?

J　2週間お待ちください。
　　Ni-shū-kan omachi kudasai.

機械・機器の修理

日本のメーカーは消費者サービスにとくに力を入れています。電気製品・カメラ・時計・事務機器など，最低1年の保証期間があり，保証書を示せば，いつでも無料でサービスしてくれます。

時計などの電池切れの場合はすぐに直りますが，カメラなど部品を交換する必要のあるものは，工場で修理しますから，1〜2週間はかかります。大型の電気製品などは出張修理してくれますが，修理実費のほかに出張料をとられます。

ものによっては買い替えたほうがよい場合があるので，あらかじめ修理にかかる費用をたずねましょう。

When will it be ready?

Use when you ask the day you can pick up your repaired things.

Dialog

F　Could you fix my camera?

J　Yes, certainly.

F　When will it be ready?

J　In about two weeks.

Repairing machines and instruments

Japanese manufacturers go t ogreat efforts to ensure that their customers get good after-sales service. Electric products, cameras, watches and office instruments have a 1-year guarantee period, and if you have your guarantee card you can have the article repaired for free.

The batteries in watches and other small appliances can easily be exchanged for new ones, though instruments like cameras, which need new parts, are repaired at a factory, and it takes 1 or 2 weeks. Big electric products can be repaired at your home, but you have to pay travel charges as well as the cost of the repair.

You should ask the cost beforehand because sometimes it's better to buy a new one.

助けて。痛いよう。

Tasukete! Itai yō.

あまりに痛くて人に訴えるときに言います。

ダイアローグ

F　助けて。痛いよう。
Tasukete! Itai yō.

J　あら，血がでてる。
Ara, chi ga deteru.

F　車にはねられた。
Kuruma ni hanerareta.

J　じっとしてて。いま救急車を呼ぶから。
Jitto shitete. Ima kyūkyūsha o yobu kara.

交通事故には十分注意を

日本では車は左側通行です。道路を渡るときは日本ではまず右を見てそして左を見ます。多くの外国は右側通行ですから，慣れた人でも油断をするとつい自国の癖がでます。注意しましょう。

交通事故にはぜったい遭ってほしくはありませんが，万一事故に遭ったらケガの手当が優先です。救急車は 119 番，警察は 110 番です。119 番にも場所を確実に伝えてください。

119 番は火事や急病人のときにも来てくれます。緊急のときでもあわてないで，何が起きたか，場所はどこか，そして名前を知らせましょう。

Help! I've been hurt.

Use when you are in severe pain and need help.

Dialog

F Help! I've been hurt.

J Oh, you're bleeding!

F I was hit by a car.

J Stay here. I'll call an ambulance immediately.

Be careful to avoid traffic accidents.

Cars drive on the left side in Japan. When you cross the street, you should look right first and then left. In most countries, cars drive on the right side, so you have to be careful not to be absentminded when you are about to cross the street, as your country practices right-hand traffic.

Hopefully, you won't have any accidents, but if you do by some chance, the first thing to do is to treat any wounds.

Dial 119 for an ambulance or 110 for the police. Describe the site of the accident as precisely as possible to the ambulance.

If there is a fire or a serious accident, you should call 119. Tell them calmly what has happened, where you are and your name.

とってもこわかった。

Tottemo kowakatta.

恐(おそろ)しい目(め)にあったことを話(はな)すときに言(い)います。

ダイアローグ

F　けさ，とってもこわかった。
　Kesa, tottemo kowakatta.

J　地震(じしん)でしょ。
　Jishin desho?

F　そう，こわくて動(うご)けなかったの。
　Sō, kowakute ugokenakatta no.

J　あら。まず火(ひ)を消(け)さなくちゃ。
　Ara. Mazu hi o kesanakucha.

広域避難場所(こういきひなんばしょ)

日本は予告(よこく)なく小(ちい)さな地震がよく起(お)こるので，都会(とかい)のビルはかなり大きな地震にも耐(た)えられるように造(つく)られています。しかし安心(あんしん)はできません。

もし大地震(おおじしん)が起(お)きたら，まず安全(あんぜん)な場所(ばしょ)に避難(ひなん)してください。どこの都市にも広域避難場所(こういきひなんばしょ)が設定(せってい)されています。公園(こうえん)，広場(ひろば)，神社(じんじゃ)，墓地(ぼち)，運動場(うんどうじょう)など指定(してい)された地域(ちいき)が屋外掲示板(おくがいけいじばん)に出ています。

地震を感(かん)じたら何はともあれ，火(ひ)の元(もと)を消(け)してください。ガスの元(もと)せん，石油(せきゆ)ストーブ，タバコの火(ひ)，いいですね。

I was so frightened.

For use when you have had a terrible experience.

Dialog

F **I was so frightened this morning.**

J **Was it an earthquake?**

F **Yes. I was sitting in the bathroom.**

J **Oh, no. Next time, go straight and turn off the gas or heaters.**

Evacuation areas

In Japan, many small earthquakes happen without warning. Japanese buildings in the cities are designed to resist earthquakes. But that doesn't mean you are totally safe.

If a really big earthquake happens, evacuate to a safe place first. All cities have specific evacuation areas. They can be parks, plazas, shrines, graves, playgrounds, etc. There are road signs indicating where to go.

When you feel an earthquake, before doing anything else, extinguish any fires. Turn off the gas, put out kerosine heaters and cigarettes.

ビザの書きかえです。

Biza no kakikae desu.

ビザの有効期間にはとくに気をつけましょう。

ダイアローグ

F　アメリカに行ってきます。
Amerika ni itte kimasu.

J　え。何しに。
E? Nani shini?

F　ビザの書きかえです。
Biza no kakikae desu.

J　あ，そう。気をつけていってらっしゃい。
A, sō. Kiotsukete itte rasshai.

出入国管理法を守ろう

ビザはこの国に入ってよろしいという証明です。したがってその証明にはいろいろな条件がついています。

現在日本では，専門的な技術や技能，知識をつかって働こうとする外国人をできるだけ受け入れるようにしていますが，入国するまえに本人か日本の受け入れ機関（会社・団体・組織）の代理人が，地方入国管理局に申請し「在留資格認定証明書」の交付を受ける必要があります。それを持たない外国人は日本で受け入れのスポンサーを見つけ，いったん出国し，その証明書を持って再入国します。

日本で働くことが許可されていない外国人を雇った日本人も厳しく罰せられます。

To renew my visa.

You should be especially careful about your visa expiry date.

Dialog

F **I'm going back to the States for a few days.**

J **Are you? What for?**

F **To renew my visa.**

J **I see. Have a safe journey.**

Observe the immigration laws!

A visa is a certificate that indicates you can enter Japan. There are many conditions attached to it. In fact, there are 28.

Japan now accepts foreigners who have special skills and knowledge. Before you enter this country, it is possible to get a certificate of authorized resident qualification. You yourself, a Japanese representative of a company or some other organization may apply at the local Immigration Office. Foreigners who don't have this certificate have to find a sponsor who will act as a guarantor for them and apply for the visa. They must leave Japan and re-enter with the certificate. Japanese who employ foreigners who do not have a work visa will be punished severely.

電車に乗り遅れました。

Densha ni nori okure mashita.

約束の時間に遅れるときは必ず電話しましょう。

ダイアローグ

J　はい，佐藤です。え。マイク。
Hai, Satō desu. E? Maiku?

F　電車に乗り遅れました。
Densha ni nori okure mashita.

J　つぎの電車は。
Tsugi no densha wa?

F　30分あとです。
Sanjippun ato desu.

引っ越しするときは

市［区］外へ引っ越しするときは，まず市役所へ行きます。英文パンフレットがあれば最初に読んで，それから窓口で転出の手続きと保険・税金についてどうしたらいいかをたずねます。電話局で電話の移転，解約の手続きもあります。また，電気・ガス・水道会社へも連絡をしましょう。

次に，荷物です。電話帳で近くの運送業者を調べ電話します。荷物の大きさと量をみて費用の見積もりをしてくれます。細かい物の荷造り用に必要なダンボール，ひも，ガムテープ，シートなども用意してくれます。

業者にまかせたら，引っ越し先で待っていて家具の置き場所などを指示しましょう。その前に大家さんや近所へのあいさつを忘れずに。

海外へ引っ越すときも大手業者がとり扱ってくれます。

I missed the train.

You should call when you are going to be late for an appointment.

Dialog

J **Hello, this is Satō speaking. Oh, is that Mike?**

F **Yes. I missed the train.**

J **What about the next train?**

F **It comes in 30 minutes time.**

When you move house.

When you move to another place outside your city (ward), you should go to your current municipal office first. If they have an English pamphlet explaining the necessary procedures, read that first, then go to the appropriate counter. The clerk will advise you about National Health Insurance and tax at the same time. You can arrange to transfer or cancel your telephone at the nearby NTT office. You have to contact the electricity, gas, and water companies as well.

To transport your belongings is the next stage. Look up the name of a moving company in the telephone directory. They will estimate the cost after checking the quantity and size of your belongings. They can provide cardboard boxes for small things, as well as the ropes, tape, etc.

Leave everything for the moving company, then go to your new place and wait there for them. Tell them where the furniture should be placed. Before you move, don't forget to call on your landlord and neighbors.

When moving overseas, big moving companies can assist you.

病院（びょういん） The hospital

受付（うけつけ）	information/admission desk
外来（がいらい）	outpatient department
初診（しょしん）	first medical examination（初診患者は new patient）
薬局（やっきょく）	pharmacy
会計（かいけい）	cashier
診察室（しんさつしつ）	consultation room
待合い室（まちあいしつ）	waiting room
内科（ないか）	internal medicine
外科（げか）	surgery
循環器科（じゅんかんきか）	cardiology
精神科（せいしんか）	psychiatry
小児科（しょうにか）	pediatrics
整形外科（せいけいげか）	orthopedics
脳神経外科（のうしんけいげか）	neurosurgery
皮膚科（ひふか）	dermatology
泌尿器科（ひにょうきか）	urology
産婦人科（さんふじんか）	obstetrics & gynecology
眼科（がんか）	ophthalmology
歯科（しか）	dentistry
耳鼻咽喉科（じびいんこうか）	ear, nose and throat specialist
放射線科（ほうしゃせんか）	radiology/X-ray department

X
便利な表現
Convenient expressions

うそー，ほんと。

Usō, honto?

若い女性がよく使います。

ダイアローグ

J　ドロシー，お昼おごってあげる。
Doroshi, ohiru ogotte ageru.

F　うそー，ほんと。
Usō, honto?

J　あら，そんな言いかたよくおぼえたね。
Ara, sonna iikata yoku oboeta ne.

F　だって，女の子がみんな言ってるもん。
Datte, onna no ko ga minna itteru mon.

四季と12か月

日本には四季があり，それぞれの季節に味わいがあります。咲く花も季節によっていろいろです。

春	3月	ぼけ，はくもくれん，れんぎょう
	4月	さくら，かいどう
	5月	つつじ，ぼたん，ふじ，ばら
夏	6月	はなしょうぶ，あじさい
	7月	すいれん，はす
	8月	さるすべり，ふよう
秋	9月	はぎ，ひがんばな，きんもくせい
	10月	ふゆざくら，こすもす
	11月	きく
冬	12月	さざんか
	1月	はぼたん
	2月	うめ，つばき，ろうばい

I can't believe it!

Young girls always say this.

Dialog

J Dorothy, I am going to treat you to lunch today!

F I can't believe it!

J Oh, where did you get such an expression?

F Young girls are always using it!

Four seasons and 12 months

Japan has four seasons. Each season has its own flavor. Various flowers bloom in each season.

Spring	March	Japanese quince, white magnolia, forsythia, weeping golden bell
	April	cherry blossom, aronia, fringed iris
	May	azalea, peony, wisteria, rose
Summer	June	iris, hydrangea
	July	water lily, lotus
	August	crape myrtle, cotton rose
Autumn	September	Japanese bush clover, cluster amaryllis, fragrant olive
	October	winter cherry blossom, cosmos
	November	chrysanthemum
Winter	December	sasanqua
	January	ornamental kale
	February	Japanese plum, camellia, Japanese allspice

わかんない。

Wakan-nai.

理由(りゆう)が説明(せつめい)できないときに言(い)います。

ダイアローグ

J　どうして学校(がっこう)へ行(い)かないの。
Dōshite gakkō e ikanai no?

F　わかんない。
Wakan-nai.

J　わかった。ホームシックなんだ。
Wakatta. Hōmu-shikku nanda.

F　ううん。
Uun.

疑問(ぎもん)の表現(ひょうげん)

なぜ，どうして…「なぜ来(こ)ないのですか」

だれ…「だれと行くのですか」

なに…「なにをしましょうか」

いつ…「いつ会いましょうか」

どこ…「どこで行われるのですか」

どうして，どうやって，どのようにして…

「どうして［どうやって，どのようにして］ここまで来(き)たのですか」

I don't know.

Use when you can't give a reason or explanation.

Dialog

J **Why don't you go to school?**

F **I don't know.**

J **I know. You're homesick, aren't you?**

F **No ....**

The expression of questions

Why	Why don't they come?
Who(m)	Who(m) are you going with?
What	What are we going to do?
When	When shall we meet?
Where	Where will it be held?
Why, how	How did you get here?

あれ，やだ。

Are, yada

自分の失敗に気がついたときなどに言います。

ダイアローグ

F　あれ，やだ。忘れ物しちゃった。
　　Are, yada. Wasuremono shichatta.

J　何を。
　　Nani o?

F　今日の宿題。
　　Kyō no shukudai.

J　取りに帰る。
　　Tori ni kaeru?

曜日と日時

曜日　月曜日，火曜日，水曜日，木曜日，金曜日，土曜日，日曜日

週　今週，先週，来週，週末，平日

祝日・祭日　記念日，誕生日

時間　1時間，1分，5分，10分，10秒，午前，午後，正午，
昼，夕方，夜，今朝，今日，今晩，昨日，おととい，明日，
午前7時30分，午後2時5分，3時10分前

Oh, no!

Use when you realize you have made a mistake and so on.

Dialog

F **Oh, no! I've left something behind.**

J **What did you forget?**

F **Today's homework.**

J **Will you go back and get it?**

Days and times

Days	Monday, Tuesday, Wednesday, Thursday, Friday, Saturday, Sunday.
Week	This week, last week, next week, weekends, weekdays.
Holiday	anniversaries, birthdays.
Times	1 hour, 1 minute, 5 minutes, 10 minutes, 10 seconds, morning, afternoon, noon, evening, night, this morning, today, this evening, yesterday, the day before yesterday, tomorrow, half past seven in themorning, 5 minutes past two in the afternoon, 10 minutes to 3 o'clock.

こんなにたくさん。

Konna ni takusan.

予期(よき)しないくらいの量(りょう)を表(あらわ)します。

ダイアローグ

J　デイブ，おたんじょうびおめでとう。
Deibu, o-tanjōbi omedetō.

F　ありがとう
Arigatō.

J　プレゼントのお花(はな)よ。
Purezento no ohana yo.

F　こんなにたくさん。いいの。
Konna ni takusan. Iino?

反対語(はんたいご)

大(おお)きい ⟷ 小(ちい)さい
長(なが)い ⟷ 短(みじか)い
軽(かる)い ⟷ 重(おも)い
まるい ⟷ 四角(しかく)い
高(たか)い ⟷ 低(ひく)い
高い ⟷ 安(やす)い
いい ⟷ わるい
きれい ⟷ きたない
好(す)き ⟷ きらい
上手(じょうず) ⟷ 下手(へた)
ほんとう ⟷ うそ
早(はや)い ⟷ 遅(おそ)い
遠(とお)い ⟷ 近(ちか)い
むずかしい ⟷ やさしい
あっち ⟷ こっち
たくさん ⟷ 少(すこ)し
うしろ ⟷ まえ
あまい ⟷ からい
行(い)き ⟷ 帰(かえ)り
いま ⟷ あと

That's a lot!

To express surprise at an unexpected amount.

Dialog

J **Happy birthday, Dave.**

F **Thank you.**

J **Here are some flowers for you.**

F **That's a lot! Are they all for me?**

Antonyms

big ⟷ small
long ⟷ short
light ⟷ heavy
round ⟷ square
high ⟷ low
expensive ⟷ cheap
good ⟷ bad
clean ⟷ dirty
like ⟷ dislike
good ⟷ bad
fact ⟷ lie
quick ⟷ slow
far ⟷ near
difficult ⟷ easy
there ⟷ here
a lot ⟷ little
back ⟷ front
sweet ⟷ sour
go ⟷ return
now ⟷ later

それは残念。

Sore wa zannen.

心残り(こころのこ)のときや悔(くや)しいときに言(い)います。

ダイアローグ

J　この間(あいだ)の写真(しゃしん)，全部(ぜんぶ)だめだった。
Konoaida no shashin, zenbu dame datta.

F　それは残念(ざんねん)。
Sore wa zannen.

J　ドリームランド，たのしかったね。
Dorimu-rando, tanoshikatta ne.

F　また行(い)こうよ。
Mata ikō yo.

なぜそんなことば知ってるの（1）

①やだー，照(て)れくさいよ。

②なんだか，ずっこけちゃう。

③今日(きょう)は，たるんでるね。

④そんなにつっぱるの，やめなさい。

⑤あいつ，ださいな。

⑥あのこ，とんでる。

⑦ぼくには，ちんぷんかんぷんだ。

⑧あなたのスーツ，ぴったりね。

⑨そんな，めちゃくちゃな。

⑩あーあ，ぐったりしちゃった。

That's a pity!

Use when you feel regret or frustration.

Dialog

J I just ruined the photograph we took the other day.

F That's a pity.

J We enjoyed the Dreamland, didn't we?

F Shall we go again?

How did you come to know these expressions?(1)

① Oh, no. I'm embarrassed.
② It's such a disappointment.
③ You're so slow today!
④ Don't be so stubborn!
⑤ He's horrible.
⑥ She's trendy.
⑦ It's just jargon.
⑧ Your suit looks good on you.
⑨ It's nonsense!
⑩ Oh, I'm dead tired!

あー，せいせいした。

Ah, seisei shita.

いやなことがすんで，さっぱりしたときに言(い)います。

ダイアローグ

F　あー，せいせいした。
　　Ah, seisei shita.

J　うれしそうだね。
　　Ureshisō dane.

F　だって，やっと試験(しけん)がすんで。
　　Datte, yatto shiken ga sunde.

J　じゃ，のびのびできるね。
　　Ja, nobinobi dekiru ne.

なぜそんなことば知ってるの（2）

①ぼちぼち始(はじ)めようか。

②あんまりがやがやしないで。

③きょうはじめじめしますね。

④どうしてそんなにつんつんしてるの。

⑤手(て)がかさかさする。

⑥もうあきあきだ。

⑦なんだか朝(あさ)からくさくさしてる。

⑧そろそろ帰(かえ)りましょう。

⑨肌(はだ)がすべすべしている。

⑩あの子のおしゃべりにはたじたじだ。

Oh, I’m so relieved.

Use when you have finished doing something difficult and you feel relieved.

Dialog

F **Oh, I’m so relieved.**

J **You do sound happy!**

F **Yes, my examinations are finished at last!**

J **You can relax now.**

How did you come to know these expressions?(2)

① Shall we do it bit by bit?
② Don’t be so noisy!
③ It’s humid today, isn’t it?
④ Why are you so cross?
⑤ My hands are dry and rough.
⑥ I’m bored.
⑦ I’ve felt depressed since this morning.
⑧ Shall we go back now?
⑨ My skin is smooth.
⑩ I was discouraged by that girl’s talk.

さっぱりした。

Sappari shita.

さわやかな気持(きも)ちになったときに言(い)います。

ダイアローグ

F　おふろに入(はい)って，さっぱりした。
　　Ofuro ni haitte, sappari shita.

J　汗(あせ)かいてるね。
　　Ase kaiteru ne.

F　ビールでも飲(の)もうか。
　　Biru demo nomō ka.

J：ぼくも床屋(とこや)に行(い)ってさっぱりした。
　　Boku mo tokoya ni itte sappari shita.

なぜそんなことば知ってるの（3）

①今夜(こんや)の月はまんまるだ。

②ふとんを干(ほ)したらふんわりした。

③もっとじっくり考えなさい。

④あいつもちゃっかりしてる。

⑤はなからできないことはわかっていた。

⑥車(くるま)がえんこした。

⑦道(みち)ですってんころり。

⑧でこぼこしてて歩きにくい。

⑨じきにおしまい。

⑩あー，しんど。

I feel refreshed.

Use when you feel refreshed.

Dialog

F I feel refreshed after taking a bath.

J You're perspiring.

F Shall we have a few beers?

J I also feel refreshed after having my hair cut.

How did you come to know these expressions?(3)

① The moon tonight is perfectly round.
② My futon's become soft and warm after being hung out in the sun.
③ Think more seriously about it!
④ He is so smart!
⑤ I know it's impossible.
⑥ My car has broken down.
⑦ I slipped on the street.
⑧ It's really hard to walk here because this road is very bumpy.
⑨ It finishes soon.
⑩ I'm tired.

体の部分名称　Parts of the human body

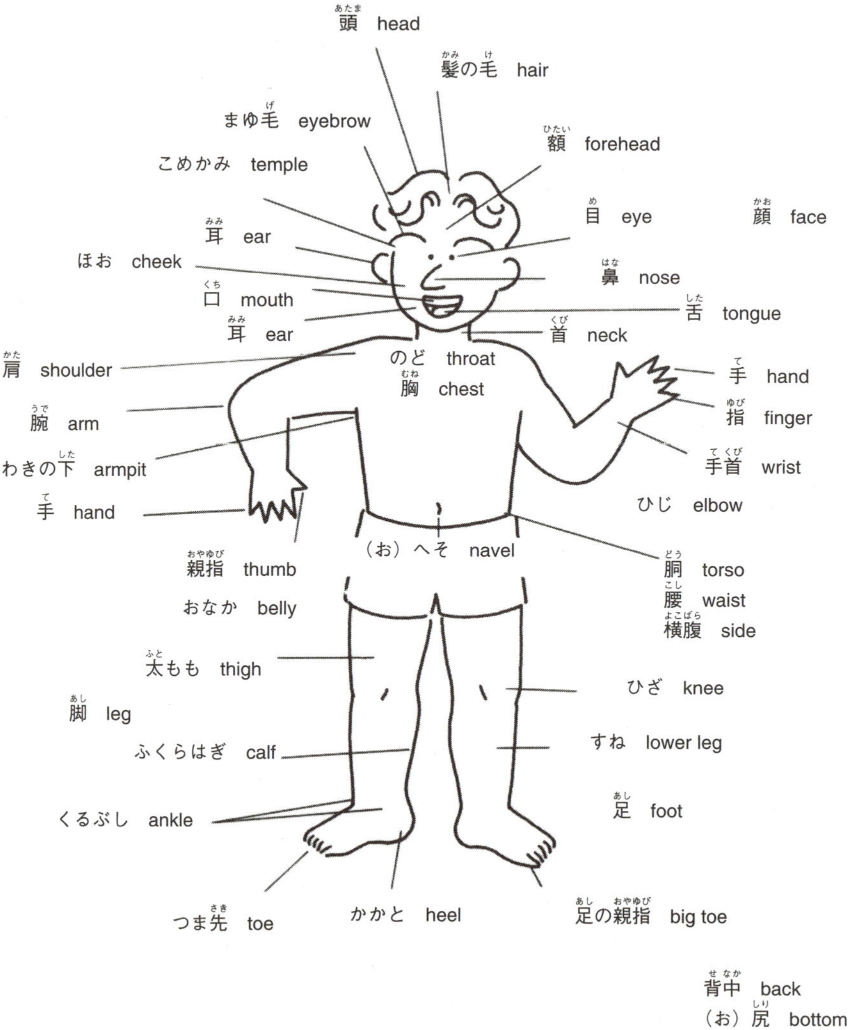

色(いろ) Colors

白(しろ) white
青(あお) blue
橙色(だいだいいろ) orange
紫(むらさき) purple
緑(みどり) green

黄色(きいろ) yellow
黒(くろ) black
ピンク pink
すみれ色(いろ) violet
金色(きんいろ) gold

赤(あか) red
灰色(はいいろ) grey
茶色(ちゃいろ) brown
水色(みずいろ) light blue
銀色(ぎんいろ) silver

日本(にほん)の年中行事(ねんちゅうぎょうじ) Annual events in each of the four seasons

正月(しょうがつ)	New Year's Day
節分(せつぶん)	the day before the beginning of spring
(節分の豆(まめ)きはthe bean scattering ceremony celebrating the coming of spring)	
ひな祭(まつ)り	the Doll's[Girls'] Festival
端午(たんご)の節句(せっく)	the Boys' Festival
七夕(たなばた)	the Star Festival
お盆(ぼん)	Lantern Festival
お彼岸(ひがん)	the equinoctial week
お月見(つきみ)	moon viewing
運動会(うんどうかい)	athletic meeting[meet]
七五三(しちごさん)	a festive day for children of three, five and seven years of age
クリスマス	Christmas
大(おお)みそか	New Year's Eve
お年玉(としだま)	New Year's gift money
お中元(ちゅうげん)	mid-year[summer] present[gift]
お歳暮(せいぼ)	year-end present[gift]

地名(ちめい)クイズ　Map Quiz

次(つぎ)の日本(にほん)の地名(ちめい)をひらがなで書(か)き，手持(ても)ちの地図(ちず)で探(さが)してみましょう。

Write the Japanese places in hiragana and find out where they located, using your maps.

1. 東京　Tokyo　(　　　　)
2. 鎌倉　Kamakura　(　　　　)
3. 箱根　Hakone　(　　　　)
4. 富士　Fuji　(　　　　)
5. 名古屋　Nagoya　(　　　　)
6. 大阪　Osaka　(　　　　)
7. 京都　Kyoto　(　　　　)
8. 奈良　Nara　(　　　　)
9. 岡山　Okayama　(　　　　)
10. 広島　Hiroshima　(　　　　)
11. 高知　Kochi　(　　　　)
12. 福岡　Fukuoka　(　　　　)
13. 長崎　Nagasaki　(　　　　)
14. 沖縄　Okinawa　(　　　　)
15. 札幌　Sapporo　(　　　　)
16. 旭川　Asahikawa　(　　　　)
17. 仙台　Sendai　(　　　　)
18. 盛岡　Morioka　(　　　　)
19. 日光　Nikko　(　　　　)
20. 軽井沢　Karuizawa　(　　　　)
21. 筑波　Tsukuba　(　　　　)
22. 三条　Sanjo　(　　　　)
23. 新潟　Niigata　(　　　　)
24. 天竜　Tenryu　(　　　　)
25. 四日市　Yokkaichi　(　　　　)
26. 神戸　Kobe　(　　　　)
27. 鳥取　Tottori　(　　　　)
28. 北九州　Kitakyushu　(　　　　)
29. 対馬　Tsushima　(　　　　)
30. 石垣島　Ishigakijima　(　　　　)

解答(かいとう)　Antworten

1. とうきょう　2. かまくら　3. はこね　4. ふじ　5. なごや　6. おおさか　7. きょうと　8. なら　9. おかやま　10. ひろしま　11. こうち　12. ふくおか　13. ながさき　14. おきなわ　15. さっぽろ　16. あさひかわ　17. せんだい　18. もりおか　19. にっこう　20. かるいざわ　21. つくば　22. さんじょう　23. にいがた　24. てんりゅう　25. よっかいち　26. こうべ　27. とっとり　28. きたきゅうしゅう　29. つしま　30. いしがきじま

カタカナクイズ　katakana-Quiz

次のカタカナを英語で書きなさい。

Translate these katakana letters into their alphabetical equivalents.

1. エブラハム・リンカーン　(　　　　　　　　　　)
2. サンフランシスコ　(　　　　　　　　　　)
3. ウィンドサーフィン　(　　　　　　　　　　)
4. マイケル・ジャクソン　(　　　　　　　　　　)
5. ウエストミンスター　(　　　　　　　　　　)
6. スペースシャトル　(　　　　　　　　　　)
7. サッカー・チーム　(　　　　　　　　　　)
8. シドニー　(　　　　　　　　　　)
9. セールス・エンジニア　(　　　　　　　　　　)
10. ポラロイド・カメラ　(　　　　　　　　　　)
11. アフリカ　(　　　　　　　　　　)
12. ヨーロッパ　(　　　　　　　　　　)
13. オーストリア　(　　　　　　　　　　)
14. フランス　(　　　　　　　　　　)
15. ミャンマー　(　　　　　　　　　　)
16. ギリシャ　(　　　　　　　　　　)
17. インド　(　　　　　　　　　　)
18. マレーシア　(　　　　　　　　　　)
19. フィリピン　(　　　　　　　　　　)
20. スウェーデン(　　　　　　　　　　)

解答　Antworten

1. Abraham Lincoln　2. San Francisco　3. wind surfing　4. Michael Jackson　5. Westminster
6. space shuttle　7. soccer team　8. Sydney　9. sales engineer　10. Polaroid 11. Africa
12. Europe　13. Austria　14. France　15. Myanmar　16. Greece　17. India
18. Malaysia　19. Philippines　20. Sweden

日本の家庭料理の作り方1

野菜の天ぷら

準備：

① 野菜（さつまいも，かぼちゃ，にんじん，なす，玉ねぎ，はす，しいたけなど）をよく洗って，それぞれ 5 mm～1 cm の厚さに切って，水分をふきとる。＊えび，白身魚，いかなどを使うのが正式な天ぷら

② 衣は，小麦粉と同量の水を混ぜ，さらに卵を加えて混ぜる。

③ 油は天ぷら油またはサラダ油 180°C(330°F～340°F)に温めておく。

料理の仕方：それぞれの野菜に衣をつけ，すぐ油の中に入れる。衣の色がきつね色になり，野菜が浮いてきたらできあがり。

盛つけ：大皿にクッキングペーパーを敷き，種類別に並べる。

食べ方：レモン汁を少しかけ，食塩で食べる。揚げたてがおいしい。

＊正式には天つゆにつけて食べるが，塩が簡単でいいでしょう。

Recipes for cooking Japanese dishes at home. 1

Vegetable tenpura

Ingredients and preparation: ①Fresh vegetables such as sweet potato, pumpkins, carrot, eggplant, onion, lotus roots, black mushrooms, etc, can be used. The vegetables should be washed and cleaned and cut into pieces of about 5 mm —1 cm in thickness. (Wipe after cutting) *Prawns, white meat fish, or cuttlefish are often used to prepare a formal style of *tenpura*. ②The coating mixture should be prepared using equal amount of flour and water, mixed with a beaten egg. ③ Use *tenpura* oil as well as salad oil and heat it up to 180°C.(300 —— 340°F)

Recipe: After dipping each of the pieces in the coating mixture, fry in the heated oil. Remove from the oil when the color of the coating turns light brown, and the vegetables rise to the surface.

Presentation: Put a sheet of absorbent paper on a large dish, and place the vegetables in rows, according to their variety, upon it.

The best way to eat tempura: *Tenpura* tastes best when eaten just after cooking. Season with salt and a squeeze of lemon juice.

*The traditional way of eating *tenpura* is to first dip the pieces, as you eat them, into a bowl of *tentsuyu* (special soup). (This can be bought in ready-made bottles from the supermarket.) However, sprinkling salt over the *tenpura* is probably easier.

日本の家庭料理の作り方2

カレーライス（4人前）

準備：

① 野菜（じゃがいも2個，にんじん1本，玉ねぎ2個）は皮をむき，それぞれ3cm角くらいに切る。

② 肉は，好みのもの（牛，豚，鳥）を200g用意し，食べやすい大きさに切る。

③ カレーのルー1パック。　④バター 1/8 ポンド。　⑤ごはん4人前。

料理の仕方：

① 大鍋を火にかけ，バターを入れ，溶けたところで野菜を全部入れて炒め，軽く火が通ったところで肉を入れてかきまわす。それに水をひたひたになるくらい注ぎ，ふたをして30分～1時間とろ火で煮る。

② いったん火を止めて，カレールーを刻んで入れ，溶けるまで軽くかきまわす。溶けたらもう一度火にかけひと煮立ちさせてできあがり。

盛つけ：

皿の半分にごはんを盛り，片側にカレーをかける。スプーンでどうぞ。

Recipes for cooking Japanese dishes at home. 2

Curry rice (4 people)

Ingredients: ① 2 medium-sized potatoes, 1 carrot, and 2 medium-sized onions, peeled and cut into chunks of about 3 cm. ② 200 grams of lean meat, (beef, pork and chicken are all suitable) to be cut into mouth-size pieces. ③ one package of instant curry roux. (available at most supermakets) ④ 1/8 pound of butter. ⑤ 4 bowls of cooked rice.

Preparation: ①Heat a large sauce pan and add the butter. When the butter melts, put all the vegetables in the pot and fry them. When the vegetables are soft, add the meat and stir the mixture. Add just enough water to cover the mixture and simmer for 30 minutes to 1 hour, with a lid on the pan. ②Turn off the burner and add the instant curry roux which has been chopped finely. Keep stirring until the instant curry roux has completely melted, forming a smooth sauce. Turn on the burner again, and bring to a boil. Reduce the heat and simmer for a few minutes.

Presentation: Place the rice on one side of each individual dinner plate, and spoon portions of the curry mixture onto the other side of the plate. Eat with a spoon.

日本語化した英語　Japlish

●自動車関係　Automobiles

ハンドル　**steering wheel**
アクセル　**accelerator pedal**
クラクション　**horn**
フロントガラス　**windshield**
タイヤ　**wheel**
バンパー　**shock absorber**
サイドブレーキ　**hand brake**
バックミラー　**rear-window mirror**
パトカー　**police car**
キャンピングカー　**camper**
サービスバス　**courtesy bus**
ダンプカー　**dump truck**
オートバイ　**motorcycle**
ガソリンスタンド　**gas station**
ドライブ　**go for a ride**

●人　Human being

ガードマン　**security guard**
テレビタレント　**TV star**
グラマー　**voluptuous woman**

●スポーツ　Sports

シーズンオフ　**off-season**
ナイター　**night game**
ビジター　**visiting team**
ハンディ　**handicap**
ファインプレー　**nice play**
バックネット　**backstop**

●住まい　Housing

クーラー　**air conditioner**
プッシュホン　**push-button phone**
リビングセット　**living room suite**
コンセント　**(wall) outlet**
ヘルスメーター　**scale**
バスマット　**rug**
アパート　**apartment house**
マンション　**apartment house**

●その他　Others

テーマ　**theme**
チャームポイント
charming point
プライスダウン　**markdown**
アフターサービス　**follow-up service**
クレーム　**complaint**
ジャンパー　**jacket**
ゴールデンアワー　**prime time**
シュークリーム　**cream puff**
ミキサー　**blender**
サイン　**signature**
ワイシャツ　**(white) shirt**